FROM THE MINES
TO THE MOUNTAINS

Other books by Stephen Matthews:

Sarah Losh and Wreay Church
The Life and Work of David Dunbar Sculptor
King Arthur lives in Merrie Carlisle
The Spectral Army of Souther Fell
Christopher at the Lakes
The Gentleman who Surveyed Cumberland
Josiah Relph of Sebergham: England's First Dialect Poet
A Lazy Tour of Cumberland
The Life and Works of David Dunbar, Sculptor
Beauty in the Lap of Horror
The Sun Shines Fair on Carlisle Wall: An Anthology of Carlisle in Literature

By Christopher Donaldson:
with Robert Dunning and Angus J.L. Winchester (eds), Henry Hobhouse's Tour Through Cumbria in 1774

Copyright: C.Donaldson; S Matthews
First edition 2018
ISBN 978-1-912181-15-5
Published by Bookcase, 19 Castle St., Carlisle, CA3 8SY
01228 544560   bookscumbria@aol.com
Printed by The Amadeus Press.

FROM THE MINES TO THE MOUNTAINS

John Dalton's *Descriptive Poem* of 1755 and Contemporary Accounts of Cumberland & Westmorland

Edited and introduced by
Christopher Donaldson and Stephen Matthews

BOOKCASE

Detail from Matthias Read's A Bird's-Eye View of Whitehaven *(c.1735)*

Contents

Preface	v
List of Illustrations	vii
Introduction	1
The Author: John Dalton (1709–1763)	3
The Text: Dalton's *Descriptive Poem* (1755)	13
The Context: Cumberland & Westmorland in Dalton's Era	27
A View of Georgian Whitehaven	27
The Lowthers & Whitehaven	35
The Spedding Brothers	42
Dr William Brownrigg (1711–1800)	51
'Sweet Keswick's Vale'	59
Lowther, Fondly 'Familiar to the Sight'	66
Editorial Method	82
Notes to the Introduction	83
***A Descriptive Poem, Addressed to Two Ladies, at their Return from Viewing the Mines near Whitehaven* (1755) by John Dalton**	97
Notes to *A Descriptive Poem*	141
Appendices	151
Appendix 1: 'A Poetical Prospect of the Coastal Town and Harbour of Workington' (1752) and 'A Poetical Prospect of Whitehaven' (1752) by James Eyre Weeks	152
Notes to Appendix 1	172
Appendix 2: *A Poetical Prospect of Keswick* (1752) by Thomas Cowper	174
Notes to Appendix 2	186
Bibliography	187
Index	197

From the Mines to the Mountains

Fig. 1.Detail from Matthias Read's View of Lowther *(c. 1725)*

Preface

This book is the product of a collaboration between the two editors, and it has been produced to support the National Trust's Tables Turned project, which is a three year programme of events exploring poetry, landscape, and community in response to the Lake District World Heritage Site inscription. The editors divided the tasks between them: Christopher Donaldson contributed the contextual notes, prepared the transcriptions, created the map, index, and bibliography, and he provided the biography of Dalton and the account of his *Descriptive Poem*; Stephen Matthews set the text, designed the cover, and he placed Dalton's poem into the context of eighteenth-century Cumberland and Westmorland.

The editors have also included (as appendices) transcriptions of three other, lesser-known poetic descriptions of scenes in Cumberland and Westmorland from the 1750s: Thomas Cowper's *Poetical Prospect of Keswick* (1752) and two poems by James Eyre Weeks: 'A Poetical Prospect of the Coastal Town and Harbour of Workington' (1752) and 'A Poetical Prospect of Whitehaven' (1752). Like Dalton's *Descriptive Poem*, these works are of interest as examples of literary appreciations of Cumberland and Westmorland before the beginning of the Romantic period, with which the region is often associated. Each of these poems deserves to be more widely read, and part of our intention in this edition has been to make them more widely available.

The copy of John Dalton's *Descriptive Poem* published here is preserved in the Jackson Library, in the Carlisle Library (Reference Number: J208). The copies of Cowper's and Weeks's poems are based on copies from the Jackson Collection (Reference Numbers: J134 and J343). The editors would like to thank Stephen

From the Mines to the Mountains

White (Carlisle Library) for his assistance with reproducing these texts. Thanks are also due to Timothy Sykes (Dacre Library), Anika Spedding (Mirehouse & Gardens), Jeff Cowton and Melissa Mitchell (Wordsworth Trust), Kath Sallabank and Lucy Cavendish (Holker Hall & Gardens), Martin Norgate and Jean Norgate (Guides to the Lakes), Nicola Lawson, Kerry McLaughlin, and Alan Irwin (The Beacon Museum, Whitehaven), and the staff at the Carlisle Records Office for providing access to materials from their collections. Christopher Donaldson also thanks the Leverhulme Trust for supporting elements of the research for this publication under Research Project Grant RPG-2015-230.

List of Illustrations

Frontispiece. Detail from Matthias Read's *Bird's-Eye View of Whitehaven* (c. 1735)	ii
Fig. 1. Detail from Matthias Read's *View of Lowther* (c.1725)	iv
Fig. 2. Map of key locations	viii
Fig. 3. St Oswald's Church, Dean	4
Fig. 4. *A Plan of the Town & Harbour of Whitehaven*, by J. Howard (1811)	20
Fig. 5. Detail from *A Plan of the Town & Harbour of Whitehaven*, by J. Howard (1811)	26
Fig. 6. Interior of St James' Church, Whitehaven	29
Fig. 7. One of the roundels in St James' Church, Whitehaven	30
Fig. 8. Jan Wyck's *View of Whitehaven from the Sea* (1686)	32
Fig. 9. 'The South East Prospect of Whitehaven in the Year 1642'	33
Fig. 10. Matthias Read's *A Bird's-Eye View of Whitehaven* (c.1735)	34
Fig. 11. A Plan of Whitehaven (c.1690)	38
Fig. 12. Detail from *Derwentwater: Sale of Timber* (c.1749)	66
Fig. 13. Thomas Smith's *Derwentwater from Crow Park* (1761)	67
Fig. 14. Johannes Kip's *Lowther in the County of Westmorland* (1707); after Leonard Knyff (1650–1722)	72
Fig.15. Matthias Read's *View of Lowther* (c.1725)	75

From the Mines to the Mountains

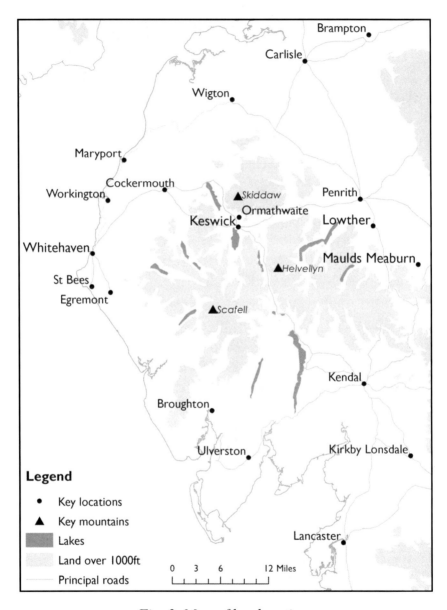

Fig. 2. Map of key locations

Introduction

Names, like books, have their own destinies. Some persist through time; most, however, are either forgotten or, if not forgotten, then eclipsed – obscured by others more noteworthy or famous. This latter lot has unfortunately befallen the once-celebrated poet and cleric John Dalton (1709–1763). A native of west Cumberland, Dalton has had the mixed blessing of sharing his name with his fellow North Countryman: the pioneering chemist, John Dalton (1766–1844). It remains a curious accident of history that these two otherwise-unrelated men should have hailed from the same county. It is all the more curious that their lives should have come so close to coinciding. Dalton, the poet, was born in Dean, near Cockermouth. Dalton, the chemist, was born just down the road, in Eaglesfield. Their birthplaces are a mere three miles apart, which is, oddly enough, the same number of years that separated their lifetimes.

Still, today, whereas most schoolchildren learn of Dalton, the chemist, comparatively few people know of Dalton, the poet. Those who do know of him, moreover, are more likely to have heard his name than to have read either his sermons or his verse. Though he was recognised as 'an eminent divine and poet' in his day, his works have been all but forgotten in our own time.[1] Yet, to him rightfully goes the honour of having helped to shape the sensibility that has made Cumbria famous the world over. Indeed, if the county contains places of outstanding universal value, then Dalton is owed a share of the credit for having helped us to perceive and to articulate that value.

Dalton's main contribution in this regard was a poem he

published in 1755: *A Descriptive Poem, Addressed to Two Ladies, at their Return from Viewing the Mines near Whitehaven*. This poem, as its lengthy title implies, is in many ways a conventional work of its period. It is composed of rhyming couplets and shot-through with references to the works of classical authors. It is, moreover, a poem conspicuously written to honour the achievements of a powerful, landholding family: the Lowthers. That is not to say, however, that it is a work without its surprises. Its descriptions of rural and urban scenery and of agricultural and industrial innovation (to say nothing of its account of subterraneous exploration) are as liable to capture the imagination of readers today as they did that of Dalton's contemporaries – many of whom were enticed by the poem to visit the places it portrays.

Frequently quoted, consulted, and reprinted, Dalton's poem gradually became a key document in the development of interest in both the industrial wonders of the west Cumberland coalfield and the dramatic mountain scenery of the county's interior. As Peter Bicknell asserts in his authoritative bibliography of Lakeland tour books, guidebooks, and picture books: Dalton's poem helped to lay 'the foundation stones of picturesque writing about the lakes'.[2] Dalton's words, that is, paved the way not only for the early visitors (such as Arthur Young, Thomas Pennant, and Thomas Gray) who are often credited with the region's 'discovery', but also for the Romantic poets whose works have helped to define perceptions of Cumbria and the Lake District for the past two-hundred years. In both of these respects, Dalton's poem has added immeasurably to the county's cultural history and its modern-day reputation.

Dalton's *Descriptive Poem* deserves to be more widely read, and not only for the sake of its historical interest. Significantly, it is also a work that speaks to the concerns of our own time. The regard it pays to both Cumbria's coastal industries and its central uplands is especially notable, as it calls attention to the arbitrariness

Introduction

of the partitioning of the county formalised in the twentieth century by, amongst other things, the creation of the Lake District National Park. It is the purpose of this edition, then, to make Dalton's poem more accessible and to contextualise it both biographically and historically. In the pages that follow, our aim is first to provide an account of Dalton's life and of his poem. From there, we shall conclude by situating Dalton's *Descriptive Poem* within the Cumberland and Westmorland of his era.

The Author: John Dalton (1709–1763)

The circumstances into which John Dalton was born were favourably disposed to support the literary and clerical career he subsequently pursued. Although little is recorded about his mother, Elizabeth (née Clarke) (c.1677–1747), his father, the Revd. John Dalton (c.1676–1729), came from a distinguished ecclesiastical family.[3] This Revd. Dalton, was a graduate of St Edmund Hall, Oxford, and a man renowned both for his learning and for his devotion to the Established Church. He served as the curate of Appleby (from 1695) and Ravenstonedale (from 1697), before being appointed Rector of Dean in 1705, and then of Distington in 1712 (Figure 3). Thereafter, in 1715, he was elected as the first minister of Holy Trinity Church, Whitehaven.[4] This illustrious career, marked by patronage and preferment, was in no small part aided by the reputation of the Revd. Dalton's forebears, particularly his father Henry (d.1709) and grandfather John (c.1600–1672), who successively held the incumbency of St Michael's Church, Shap.[5] This latter John Dalton, who graduated from Queen's College, Oxford, in 1619, was the famous one-eyed (or 'peed') preacher of Shap humorously commemorated in Nicolson and Burn's W*estmorland and Cumberland*.[6]

The eldest of his parent's four sons, our John Dalton (1709–1763) had the advantage of receiving his early education under the

Fig.3. St Oswald's Church, Dean

instruction of William Wilkinson at Lowther College.[7] Wilkinson (1685–1751), a native of Crosby Ravensworth, was a distinguished classicist, as well as a graduate of Queen's College, Oxford, and under his instruction Dalton and his fellow pupils cultivated the knowledge of Greek and Latin required for the pursuit of university studies. Endowed as an academy for the 'gentlemen's sons' of Cumberland and Westmorland in 1697, Lowther College was evidently a respected institution that drew pupils from a wide area.[8] The journal of Sir John Clerk (1676–1755), who enrolled his son at Lowther in 1730, affords a notable contemporaneous account of the school, which he describes as 'a large building containing two great halls and twenty-two rooms for schollars [sic]', who 'are educated in Greek and Latine [sic] for the university and are commonly eighteen years of age before they leave the school.'[9]

Introduction

In this latter respect, Dalton proved himself to be precocious. He matriculated at Queen's College, Oxford when he was just sixteen. This was not an entirely unprecedented age at which to be 'sent up' to university in the 1720s. (The philosopher David Hume's enrolment at the University of Edinburgh at the age of eleven in 1723 was far more extraordinary.) Still, Dalton's relatively early entry into Queen's College proved the beginning of a university career that would see him appointed B.A. in 1730, M.A. in 1734, College Fellow in 1741, and then, finally, B.D. & D.D. in 1750.[10]

From its foundation, Queen's College had given preference to applicants from Cumberland and Westmorland, and these old county ties were particularly strong during Dalton's lifetime. The College, consequently, attracted many of his former schoolmates at Lowther, including such influential figures as Humphrey Senhouse II (1705–1770), the founder of Maryport, who later supported Dalton's candidacy to become College Provost in the 1750s.[11] Accordingly, as much as Dalton's time at Lowther and Oxford enhanced his education, it also afforded him the chance to make lasting connections with members of the great and good of his native region. Having this opportunity was particularly essential for a man of Dalton's social standing. As a scholar from a respectable but middling family, his future prospects depended on his ability to secure the support of sufficiently powerful patrons.

Dalton was fortunate in this respect. For, not long after completing his B.A., he attached himself to the family of Charles Seymour, the Sixth Duke of Somerset (1662–1748). Seymour had acquired estates at Cockermouth and Egremont as a consequence of his marriage to Elizabeth Percy (1667–1722) in 1682, and so it is possible that Dalton may have come to his attention on account of their respective west Cumberland connections. What is certain, however, is that by the mid-1730s Dalton had become the tutor of the Duke's grandson: George Seymour, Viscount Beauchamp (1725–

1744), the son of Algernon Seymour, Earl of Hertford (1684–1750) and Frances (née Thynne), Countess of Hertford (1699–1754).

Dalton's involvement with the Seymour family proved to be of lasting importance. The Earl of Hertford, who inherited his father's title and estates in 1748, turned out to be an especially significant ally, as he eventually secured Dalton's appointment as a canon of Worcester Cathedral in 1748 and as rector of St Mary-at-Hill, London in 1749. More immediately, though, Dalton's relationship with the Seymours helped him to further his literary pursuits. The Countess of Hertford was a respected poetess and literary patron whose list of clients included John Dyer (1700–1757), Robert Dodsley (1704–1764), and William Shenstone (1714–1763).[12] These men, although no longer household names, were nonetheless among the more celebrated writers of their era. Dodsley, in particular, was a towering figure on the London literary scene, especially after he established himself as a publisher and bookseller during the mid-1730s. Crucially, though, like Dyer and Shenstone, and dozens of other aspiring writers, he had profited from the Countess's patronage early in his career.

Dalton clearly benefitted from her support as well, and from her connections with individuals such as Dodsley, who assisted Dalton with the publication of a poem he composed shortly after entering the Seymours' service: *An Epistle to a Young Nobleman from his Preceptor* (1736). This work is a moralistic meditation in the form of an open letter addressed to Dalton's young pupil (Viscount Beauchamp), and it will likely strike most modern readers as rather ponderous and didactic. But it won the praise of Dalton's contemporaries, including members of the Seymour circle, such as the hymn writer Isaac Watts (1674–1748), who went so far as to declare the *Epistle* superior to Alexander Pope's *Imitations of Horace* (1733–1738).[13]

This was, in short, a sunny period in Dalton's early life: one

Introduction

marked by achievement and recognition. It was not, however, an era without its shadows. For in addition to bringing him the regard of established poets, such as Watts, the acquaintances Dalton made during his time in the Seymours' household also occasioned the only reported scandal of his career: his reputed affair with the Countess of Hertford's friend, the poetess Henrietta Knight, Lady Luxborough (1699–1756). Our evidence for this indiscretion mainly consists of a prurient bit of gossip passed from Horace Walpole (1717–1797) to Anne Fitzpatrick, the Countess of Upper Ossory (1737/8–1804) some decades later. According to Walpole, 'Lady Luxborough … fell in love with Parson Dalton for his poetry, and they rhymed together till they chimed'.[14] Walpole was mischievously fond of scandals, and he elsewhere insinuated that the Countess of Hertford also had a dalliance with Dalton.[15] Still, there seems little reason to doubt Walpole's claims about Dalton and Knight. Her husband Robert Knight (1702–1772) certainly thought she had slept with Dalton, and banished her to his Warwickshire estate, Barrells Hall, where she is reported to have given birth to an illegitimate daughter in 1736. She remained in exile for the rest of her life.[16]

Eighteenth-century society was, by and large, inequitable in its judgements of sexual indiscretion; women, almost invariably, bore the brunt of the blame. Thus, whereas Lady Luxborough's reputation was permanently damaged, Dalton seems to have survived this brush with disgrace without dishonour. Certainly, rumours of the affair did nothing to dampen the success of his acclaimed adaptation of John Milton's masque *Comus* in 1738. This adaptation was the result of a collaboration with the celebrated composer Thomas Arne (1710–1778), and it proved undoubtedly the most successful literary undertaking of Dalton's career. It has been estimated that Dalton's libretto was reprinted 'at least forty times' before the end of the century, during which period the work was performed on hundreds of occasions.[17] Consequently, Dalton and Arne's rendition of *Comus* has come to be regarded as a pivotal work in English literary history. It not only popularised Milton's masque, but also accelerated his canonisation as a national poet.[18]

Crucially, the acclaim the work received also put Dalton in the public spotlight, and it earned him the esteem of litterateurs ranging from Charles Burney (1726–1814) to Christopher Smart (1722–1771). Even more than this, though, the adaptation brought Dalton to the attention of some of the great luminaries of the age, including the actor David Garrick (1717–1779) and the critic Samuel Johnson (1709–1784). Indeed, in 1750 Garrick and Johnson supported Dalton in staging a benefit performance of the masque for Milton's granddaughter Elizabeth Foster (c.1688–1754), who was then 'oppressed both by age and penury'.[19] It is widely reported that the charitable proceeds this performance raised amounted to £130: a sum equivalent to approximately £15,000 in terms of purchasing power today.[20]

Dalton's *Comus* was, in short, a coup, and it elevated him to the status of a minor literary celebrity. His success, however, did not estrange him from the Seymour family, in whose household he remained until 1744, when Viscount Beauchamp died of smallpox while making the Grand Tour.[21] Beauchamp's death came as a tremendous blow to the Seymour family, and Dalton chose to make a public expression of his grief by issuing a new edition of his *Epistle to a Young Nobleman* in 1745. Not inconsequently, Dalton also used this edition to affirm his enduring gratitude to the Seymours by including a second epistle, 'Addressed to the Right Honourable the Countess of Hartford'.[22] This poem is merely an amusing trifle, but its publication helped Dalton maintain the family's support and esteem. That the Earl of Hertford later helped to secure Dalton's church appointments in Worcester and London confirms that Dalton continued to enjoy the Seymours' good graces even after he left their service.

But the Seymours were not the only elite family with whom Dalton maintained meaningful connections during this period. Although the available evidence is fragmentary, it is reasonably clear that around this time Dalton was also developing or maintaining his connections with influential families in his native region – not least the Senhouses and the Lowthers. As we shall see, members of these two families lent support to Dalton during the 1740s and 1750s, when he was actively pursuing new professional opportunities in the Church and at Oxford University.

Dalton, it will be recalled, became a fellow of Queen's College in 1741, and he thereafter took Holy Orders in accordance with the College's Statutes. Having distinguished himself as a talented writer during the previous decade, he now began to prove himself a gifted orator and preacher as well. Consequently, most of the works he published during this period were sermons rather than poems. Some of these works, such as his *Sermon Preach'd at the Abbey-Church at Bath, for Promoting the Charity and Subscription Towards the General Hospital or Infirmary of that City, on Sunday, December 8, 1745*, were delivered in support of charitable causes; others, such as his *Two Sermons Preached before the University of Oxford, at St. Mary's, on Sept. 15th, and Oct. 20th, 1745*, sought to provide moral and spiritual counsel to university students; whereas others, such as his *Sermon Preached before the University of Oxford, at St Mary's, on the 5th of November, 1747*, extolled the righteousness of Protestantism and, more especially, the Established Church. Each of these sermons were later republished in Dalton's collection *Discourses on Several Subjects and Occasions* (1757), which received a number of glowing reviews in the periodical press. Tobias Smollett's journal, the *Critical Review*, for instance, advised that the collection had 'indeed but one fault …, viz. that it is too short'.[23]

But Dalton's ecclesiastical activities during this period were not confined to delivering sermons at Oxford and, on invitation, to congregations in fashionable resort towns, such as Bath. Around this time, he also found himself employed at St. James's Church, Westminster as assistant preacher to Thomas Secker (1693–1768), Bishop of Oxford (1737–1758) and, thereafter, Archbishop of Canterbury (1758–1768). Such an appointment was obviously an enviable one for an Oxford don, and it reflects not only the esteem in which Dalton's powers of oratory were held, but also the depth of his professional ambitions.

This latter aspect of Dalton's character also manifested around this time through his attempts to mobilise support for his candidacy for the Provostship of Queen's College. It was this endeavour that led Dalton to solicit the assistance of both the Lowthers and Senhouses. Specifically, it emboldened him to request the Countess of Hertford's cousin Katherine Lowther (née Pennington) (1712–1764) to urge Humphrey Senhouse II to persuade his cousin, Joseph Richmond (c.1719–1816), a recently minted fellow of Queen's College, to cast his vote for Dalton.[24]

The record of this episode is preserved in a sheaf of correspondence now in the papers of the Senhouse family in the Carlisle Records Office. These papers make it perfectly clear that both Katherine Lowther and Humphrey Senhouse were happy to use their influence in Dalton's favour. At the same time, however, these papers show that Richmond proved rather more non-committal. He demurred from pledging to give his vote to Dalton and drew attention to the College's Statutes, which, he insisted, forbid 'making any Promise or entering into any Engagements beforehand in a Case of this Nature'.[25] Instead, Richmond merely assured Senhouse that if Dalton were to be 'judg'd the worthiest Candidate' when a 'Vacancy of the Provostship' occurred, then there was 'no Question but' the vote would 'be determin'd in his

Introduction

Favour'.[26] In the end, though, Richmond decided to back another candidate. Dalton did stand for election as Provost in 1757, but he failed to receive a single vote.[27]

On one level, this sequence of events demonstrates that there were limits to the extent of the influence that even powerful, landed families could exert on the members of Oxford colleges. On another level, though, it also affirms that although Dalton's professional commitments inclined him to reside in the south throughout almost the entirety of his adulthood, he nonetheless maintained a network of supportive friends and patrons in Cumberland and Westmorland. The family of Katherine Lowther, the second wife of Robert Lowther (1681–1745) of Maulds Meaburn, appears to have been especially dear to Dalton, and he seems to have been on friendly terms with Katherine and her children: including her daughters Margaret (1733–1800), Katherine (1735–1809), and Barbara (1739–1805), and her sons Robert (1741–1777) and James, the future 1st Earl of Lonsdale (1736–1802). It is reasonably clear from the family's correspondence, at any rate, that Dalton was a familiar of their household during the mid-1750s.[28]

In developing a relationship with the Lowthers of Maulds Meaburn, Dalton was actually extending a connection of longstanding significance in his family. The Daltons appear to have been in the service of the Lowthers as far back as the mid-fifteenth century, when one John Dalton is recorded as having served as the family chaplain of Hugh Lowther VII (c.1435–1475).[29] Dalton's grandfather and great-grandfather, moreover, both held their livings in Shap at the Lowthers' pleasure, and his own father, the Revd. Dalton, owed his appointment at Holy Trinity Church to the powerful and wealthy Sir James Lowther, 4th Baronet of Whitehaven (1673–1755).[30] Sir James, the second cousin of Katherine Lowther's husband Robert, was the member of the extended Lowther family most deeply connected to the civic expansion and industrial development of Whitehaven during the eighteenth century. For Dalton, who spent a portion of his youth in the bustling port town, Sir James commanded admiration and esteem. Not inconsequently, Dalton made a point of celebrating Sir James's contributions to Whitehaven in his *Descriptive Poem*, which (as we explain below) appears to commemorate a tour of the Lowther collieries undertaken by two of Katherine Lowther's daughters sometime during the year 1753.

Little of Dalton's personal life during his last fifteen years is recorded. But one catches glimpses of him in the correspondence of members of London's literary society, including the letters of the Bluestockings. A crucial development here appears to have been his interest in acquiring a wife. Having attained sufficient financial security through the income from his Worcester prebendary and his London living, Dalton seems to have made a proposal of marriage to the poetess Elizabeth Carter (1717–1806) during the Winter of 1748/49, but he was refused. It has been suggested that Elizabeth had caught wind of Dalton's questionable relationship with Lady Luxborough. The truth of the matter, though, is that Carter's reasons for refusing Dalton's proposal remain unclear.[31] What is certain, however, is that Dalton did not take long to mend his heart. On 26 February 1749/50 he married Mary Gosling (d. after 1791), a sister of Sir Francis Gosling, a London banker and alderman.[32]

Dalton's health seems to have been in decline by the early 1760s. Once again, the available evidence is slight, but a letter that the essayist Catherine Talbot wrote to Dalton's former love interest, Elizabeth, in 1762 suggests that he was afflicted with some form of wasting illness or palsy. 'Some days since', records Talbot, 'I saw poor Dr Dalton; he is grown a mere shadow, cannot walk a step, and has but little use of his hands; however, he seems well, and talks as cheerfully and as much as ever.'[33] The scene Talbot

Introduction

depicts in her letter is not, however, a wholly melancholy one, as she also notes the 'genuine joyousness' with which Dalton's 'charming wife', Mary, applied herself in attending to her husband's needs: 'She conceals under a laughing countenance the most assiduous cares' and 'makes him forget that he has any complaints, and seems quite happy herself in a life that would wear down any body [sic] else'.[34] This touching domestic portrait affords us our final glimpse of Dalton. He died less than a year later, on 22 July 1763, and was buried in the crypt at Worcester Cathedral, where a memorial to him survives unto this day.

The Text: Dalton's *Descriptive Poem* (1755)

The news of Dalton's death was not widely reported. *The Gentleman's Magazine* printed a one-line obituary in its instalment for July 1763, and the following month the *Royal Magazine* recorded that 'the place and dignity' of Dalton's prebendary at Worcester had been reassigned.[35] Otherwise, little notice was taken of Dalton's passing in the press. His sermons and, more especially, his adaptation of *Comus* helped to keep his name alive though, and by 1784 a summary of his career had appeared in the pages of the *New and General Biographical Dictionary*. This summary is little more than a thumbnail sketch. But in addition to tallying Dalton's achievements and the titles of his more famous works, it also draws attention to a poem of his that had then begun to be more widely read: *A Descriptive Poem, Addressed to Two Ladies, at their Return from Viewing the Mines near Whitehaven*.

    This poem was first published as a quarto pamphlet in 1755, and it initially appears to have won the approval of a limited but appreciative readership. Few reviews of the poem were printed, but those that were printed proved favourable.[36] By the 1780s, however, Dalton's *Descriptive Poem* had garnered the interest and attention of a much broader audience. This development can be attributed to a number of causes, not least the inclusion of the poem in fashionable anthologies such as George Pearch's continuation of Robert Dodsley's *Collection of Poems*, which went through four editions between 1768 and 1783.[37] Chiefly, though, the increasing notoriety of Dalton's poem during this period was a consequence of the way the style and subject of the work complemented the aesthetic inclinations of the age. This was the heyday of the picturesque movement, when pictorially composed and emotionally laden representations of actual and imagined places were in demand.[38] It was also, not inconsequently, the period when the mines and mountains of Cumberland and Westmorland became objects of widespread curiosity.

Dalton's *Descriptive Poem*, which combines lyrical depictions of the collieries of Whitehaven, the designed landscape of Lowther Hall, and the comparatively less-cultivated Vale of Keswick, has long been regarded as an early specimen of picturesque writing about the region. Bicknell, in his bibliography, labels the poem 'the earliest published description of Lake District scenery in picturesque terms', and most scholars have followed his lead in grouping Dalton alongside a handful of writers, including John Brown and Thomas Cowper, who also penned aesthetically charged descriptions of Cumberland and Westmorland around this time.[39] Like these other early accounts of the two counties, Dalton's *Descriptive Poem* can be appreciated as a precursor to the writings of figures such as William Gilpin (1724–1804), who helped to further the vogue for picturesque tourism in the Lakes during the final quarter of the eighteenth century. It would be wrong, however, to assume that the importance of Dalton's poem merely consists in its status as a forerunner of the works of other authors. The poem is also interesting as an example of the literary sensibilities of its era, particularly in its adherence to the conventions of picturesque description.

Introduction

Dalton's poem appeals to the idioms of the picturesque in two distinctive ways. Occasionally, he uses specific aesthetic terms to draw attention to the psychological effects of the scenery he is describing. Hence, his memorable assessment of the awe-inspiring 'horrors' of Lodore Falls, near Derwentwater: 'Horrors like these at first alarm, | But soon with savage grandeur charm | And raise to noblest thought the mind'.[40] At other times, however, the picturesque aspect of Dalton's poem consists in his use of classical allusions and dramatic exaggerations. The effect of these stylistic decisions has struck some modern readers as *de trop*. Notably, in his seminal study of Lakeland tourism, Norman Nicholson dismissed Dalton's poem as a 'cartload of picturesque bric-à-brac'.[41] Myra Reynolds, for her part, was even more strident, and chose to summarise her opinion of the poem in three words: 'long, rambling, tedious'.[42]

Such assertions are not baseless. There are certainly portions of Dalton's poem that might strike modern readers as prolix, pompous, or obtuse. But the claims of commentators such as Nicholson and Reynolds seem to neglect the fact that Dalton's *Descriptive Poem* is hardly a wholly serious literary effort. True, there are parts of the poem that earnestly praise the industrial and commercial enterprise of specific individuals, most notably members of the Lowther family. On the whole, though, the tone of Dalton's poem veers more towards the comedic and the whimsically urbane. Several passages are overtly parodic and deploy the routines of mock-epic in a manner reminiscent of Pope's *Rape of the Lock* (1712–1717). Consider, for example, the outlandish description of the 'sooty collier' in lines 65–70:

> Agape the sooty collier stands,
> His axe suspended in his hands
> His Æthiopian teeth the while
> "Grin horrible a ghastly smile,"

> To see two goddesses so fair
> Descend to him from fields of air.⁴³

These lines are underpinned by a preposterous mixture of literary allusion and elevated diction. The quotation, 'Grin horrible a ghastly smile', bathetically recalls Milton's description of Death in the second book of *Paradise Lost*.⁴⁴ Such an appeal to the epic tradition is hardly an attempt at high seriousness; rather, it is a waggish display of erudition that seems to insist on the poem's status as a work of light but instructive entertainment.

Many of Dalton's contemporaries seem to have been satisfied to enjoy his poem on these terms. The *Monthly Review* declared the work to be both 'entertaining' and 'very poetical'.⁴⁵ Similarly, the *Gentleman's Magazine* commended the 'novelty' and 'curiosity' of Dalton's descriptions of the distinctive localities depicted in his poem.⁴⁶ As such assessments suggest, Dalton's engagement with these settings was well-suited to an audience whose taste was informed by a commitment to picturesque aesthetics. Consequently, it comes as little surprise that, as the eighteenth century wore on, Dalton's *Descriptive Poem* was taken up by an increasing number of readers who shared his interest in the industrial improvements and natural phenomena of his native region.

The estimation of the poem provided by early Lakeland tourists such as Henry Hobhouse of Hadspen House, Somerset (1742–1792) is indicative. Writing to his fiancée about Keswick in the summer of 1774, Hobhouse observed that he was 'saved the trouble' of waxing lyrical on the local scenery by 'a poem of Dr. Dalton's who has described [the vicinity] with no middling beauty'.⁴⁷ Inevitably, of course, not everyone expressed such unqualified admiration of Dalton's work. Thomas Amory (c.1691–1788), for one, found that Dalton's verses fell short of the beauty of the places they depicted, and he took the opportunity to make his opinion known in the second volume of his eccentric travel narrative *The Life of John Buncle* (1766).[48] Still, whether or not visitors to Cumberland and Westmorland considered Dalton's descriptions to be up to snuff, the fact that his poem was being mentioned in this manner affirms its increasing centrality within the expanding body of writing about the counties that accumulated over the latter half of the eighteenth century.

Quotations from and references to Dalton's *Descriptive Poem* appeared in many of the more noteworthy accounts of the region published in this period, including topographical studies such as Nicolson and Burn's *Westmorland and Cumberland* (1777) and William Hutchinson's *History of the County of Cumberland* (1794). The reprinting of Dalton's poem in these works helped to widen the dissemination of his words. Of particular importance in this respect, though, was the inclusion of Dalton's poem in publications specifically intended for Lakeland tourists, such as Thomas West's *Guide to the Lakes* (1778), which printed a portion of Dalton's poem among the extracts appended to the volume from its second edition onwards.[49]

The appearance of Dalton's poem in this latter context is especially noteworthy. West's *Guide* was an extremely influential and successful publication. The book was regularly revised and reissued between the late 1770s and the early 1820s, during which time, as Bicknell has surmised, 'it was carried by almost every visitor to the Lakes'.[50] The inclusion of Dalton's verses in such a work placed his poem alongside other texts, such as John Brown's *Description of the Lake at Keswick* (c.1753), which tourists were encouraged to regard as standards of proper taste. In short, by the time the Lakes had become a fashionable destination for tourists, Dalton's *Descriptive Poem* was recognised as an expression of the sensibility by which the region was to be appreciated and enjoyed.

The fact that visitors to the Lake District should have devoted such attention to a poem largely concerned with the town of Whitehaven may come as a surprise to some modern readers. Whitehaven is not a place many people associate with Cumbria's tourist attractions today. During Dalton's lifetime, though, the situation could not have been more different. Whitehaven was, then, a thriving commercial centre. A planned community laid out under the supervision of the Lowther family, it was the very model of a modern English town: prosperous, industrious, and orderly in its design. As much as the fells of central Cumbria, it was consequently a place that attracted travellers from near and far.

As early as the 1720s Daniel Defoe (1660–1731) characterised Whitehaven as a place of 'considerable' prowess 'for shipping off Coals', and he noted how the wealth generated 'by the Coal Trade' had begun to bring new forms of 'Merchandizing' to the town.[51] This influx of commerce found material expression in the architectural development of Whitehaven during the early decades of the eighteenth century, which earned the town a reputation for 'being one of the handsomest in the north of England'.[52] John Crofts, of Bristol (fl.1740–60) certainly agreed with this sentiment. He urged that Whitehaven should be visited, if only for the sake of the attractiveness of its civil engineering: 'You will be struck with the good appearance of Whitehaven at your approach; and more so, when you enter it, with the regularity of the streets and goodness of the buildings; the ornaments of which are of a beautiful red free-stone.'[53] Comparable assessments of the town can be found in the accounts of a wide variety of later travellers, ranging from the tour books of the Welsh naturalist Thomas Pennant (1726–1798) to the diaries of Jabez Maud Fisher (1750–1779), a Quaker from Philadelphia, who judged Whitehaven to be 'a place in point of Regularity inferior to none in the kingdom …. The Streets are well paved, the houses neat and well built', the 'Collieries … wrought to the greatest advantage'.[54]

Introduction

Fisher's reference to Whitehaven's collieries is noteworthy, as these were as crucial to the town's attractiveness to tourists as its spacious, grid-iron streets and its sandstone buildings (Figure 4). When Fisher's fellow Philadelphian Benjamin Franklin (1706–1790) travelled to Whitehaven in 1772, he made a point of touring the pits and he was impressed not only by their depth, but also by the geological insights they afforded.[55] Other visitors, including Pennant and Hobhouse were also wowed by the wonders of the mines, and they each drew attention to the state-of-the-art technology being employed both above and below ground. Of particular interest in this context were new inventions, such as the 'steel-mill' lantern devised by Carlisle Spedding (1695–1755), who served as the steward of Whitehaven's collieries from the early 1730s. This contraption, which Hobhouse and Pennant both describe in detail, used a system of hand-rotated steel wheels and cogs to repeatedly strike against a flint and thus to emit a shower of sparks which could provide illumination underground. This illumination would have been faint and flickering, but it had another advantage. The colour of the sparks was said to be a useful indicator of the extent to which firedamp was present in the air. This mill, further developed, was used as a safety device in the mines until it was replaced by the safety lamp credited to Sir Humphrey Davy (1778–1829) in 1815.

That tourists who came to Cumberland and Westmorland to explore the lakes and mountains took notice of these kinds of technological innovations affirms an aspect of eighteenth-century culture which is too often overlooked: namely, that the vogue for picturesque aesthetics was coextensive with a wide-reaching commitment to the ideals of progress and improvement in all domains of the arts and sciences. Appreciating this connection is important for forming a fair assessment of Dalton's *Descriptive Poem*, which also celebrates the ingenuity of inventions such as the

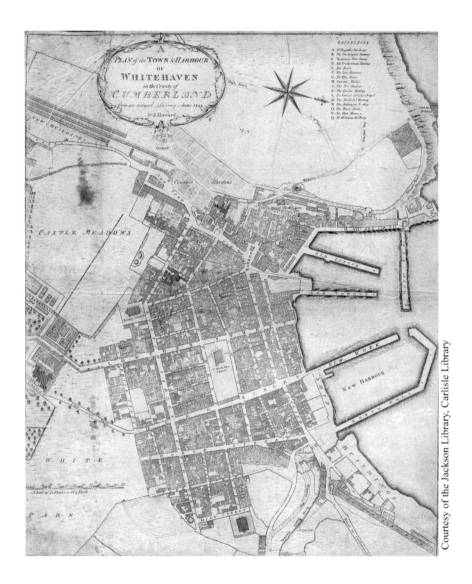

Fig.4. A Plan of the Town & Harbour of Whitehaven, by J. Howard (1811)

Introduction

Spedding mill, and, moreover, affirms its author's convictions about the essential interconnectedness of commerce, prosperity, and beauty.

One needs look no farther for evidence of this aspect of Dalton's poem than the 'Preface' he prefixed to it. Here, Dalton openly acknowledges that his verses were, in part, occasioned by 'the pleasure he had received, in a visit paid to his native country',[56] from observing the progress of various agricultural and industrial 'improvements', and more particularly 'the extraordinary' growth of Whitehaven. Witnessing these developments, Dalton explains, had left him both 'satisfied' and awe-struck:

> When we behold rich improvements of a wild and uncultivated soil, in their state of maturity, without having observed their rise and progress, we are struck with wonder and astonishment, to see the face of Nature totally changed. ... But how great and rational soever the pleasure of such a sight may be, it is still surpassed by that arising from the extraordinary increase of a trading Town, and the new plantations of Houses and Men. Such was the satisfaction the author felt at the appearance of the town and harbour of Whitehaven, after an absence of somewhat less than thirty years.[57]

Expressions of the contentment and awe Dalton describes in this passage recur throughout his poem, especially in its treatment of the wealth brought to west Cumberland through the expansion of its collieries. Of particular interest in this regard is the account of Whitehaven's ascendancy from a small coastal village to a populous port town in lines 161–72. In a manner reminiscent of Adam's vision of human history in the eleventh book of *Paradise Lost*, Dalton leads his reader into the hills above Whitehaven to trace the town's rise and progress:

> ... with an easy eye look down

From the Mines to the Mountains

On that fair port and happy town.

> Where late along the naked strand,
> The fisher's cot did lonely stand,
> And his poor bark unshelter'd lay,
> Of every swelling surge the prey,
> Now lofty piers their arms extend,
> And with their strong embraces bend
> Round crowded fleets, which safe defy
> All storms that rend the wintry sky,
> And bulwarks beyond bulwarks chain
> The fury of the roaring main.
> The peopl'd vale fair dwellings fill,
> And lengthening streets ascend the hill[.][58]

Having thus surveyed these material expressions of Whitehaven's expansion, Dalton then bursts forth to proclaim the source from which the town's prosperity stems:

> These are the glories of the mine!
> Creative Commerce, these are thine!

Modern readers might baulk at this double exclamation, with its jubilant celebration of carbon capitalism. For Dalton's contemporaries, though, this poetic encomium on the glories of industrialised fossil fuel extraction helped to place the poem within a recognisable literary pedigree. Poetry descriptive of places connected with notable events and individuals (what Dr Johnson would later dub 'local poetry') was familiar to English readers from as early as John Denham's *Cooper's Hill* (1642).[59] Closer to Dalton's day, moreover, this sort of descriptive verse had come into fashion through the success of Pope's *Windsor-Forest* (1713) and James Thompson's highly influential series *The Seasons* (1726–1730). Dalton's *Descriptive Poem*, by virtue of its very title, invoked the precedence of such works. Significantly, though, the poem also drew on the conventions of the georgic.

The georgic mode, of course, possessed an illustrious pedigree, as it originated in the works of classical authors such as Virgil (c.70–19 BCE) and Claudian (c.370–404), both of whom Dalton mentions in his 'Preface'. Georgic poetry, as the name implies, traditionally referred to the description of agricultural labour in verse. In the eighteenth century, however, the georgic underwent a considerable broadening of scope and developed into a mode suited to the literary depiction of various forms of industry – ranging from bricklaying to textile milling to coal mining. Indeed, before Dalton began his *Descriptive Poem*, the suitability of coal pits as a subject for georgic verse had been tested in Thomas Yalden's 'To Sir Humphry Mackworth: On the Mines, Late of Sir Carbery Price' (1710) and in James Eyre Weeks's 'A Poetical Prospect of the Coastal Town and Harbour of Workington' (1752) and 'A Poetical Prospect of Whitehaven' (1752).

As David Fairer has observed, georgic poems tend 'to look beneath efficient systems at the mechanisms that are at work' within them.[60] Dalton's poem certainly dwells on the industrial innovations that had helped the collieries at Whitehaven prosper. He makes a point of celebrating the ingenuity of local figures such as Spedding, whom Dalton stylises in the guise of Shakespeare's enchanter, Prospero. He describes Spedding's 'strange spark-emitting wheel, | Which, formed by Prospero's magic care, | Plays harmless in the sulphurous air'.[61] Dalton apologises for indulging in these sorts of literary exaggerations, which he justifies as the products of 'an imagination glowing warm with classical enthusiasm'.[62] His text makes up for such poetically dressed-up descriptions through the extensive footnotes supplied to it by William Brownrigg, FRS (1711–1800), the esteemed physician and chemist who we discuss at greater length below. For now, it suffices to observe that these notes explain the scientific wonders described in the poem in more technical and precise detail, and that they form a parallel text to Dalton's verse.

Descriptive poems were often written to curry favour with wealthy patrons, and Dalton's poem is no exception. Like the verse *Epistles* he penned during his time in the service of Algernon and Frances Seymour, Dalton's *Descriptive Poem* is an overt attempt to convey his friendship and admiration for a powerful, landed family: the Lowthers. Specifically, the poem affirms Dalton's relationship with the family of Robert Lowther, of Maulds Meaburn (1681–1745). Formerly a MP and the Governor of Barbados (1711–1720), Robert was a scion of the Westmorland side of the Lowther family who had acquired his considerable wealth and rank in the West Indies through his marriage to his first wife, Joan Frere (d.1722). In 1730, he added to his Westmorland holdings through the acquisition of estates including Shap, the parish from which Dalton's forebears hailed. Dalton, as noted above, appears to have been on close terms with Robert's second wife, Katherine, whose son, James Lowther (1736–1802) inherited wealth, titles, and estates from his second cousin Henry Lowther, 4th Baronet of Lowther and 3rd Viscount Lonsdale (1694–1751) and, thereafter, from his distant cousin Sir William Lowther, 3rd Baronet of Marske (1727–1756).

The anonymous addressees (the 'Two Ladies') of Dalton's poem are evidently two of Katherine's daughters. Some confusion about this matter exists, though, partly as a consequence of the notice added in Pearch's edition of the poem, which indicated the two ladies to be 'Miss Lowthers, daughters of the late Lord Lonsdale'.[63] This implies that the ladies are the daughters of Sir Henry Lowther, which is neither possible nor consistent with the content of the poem itself. Sir Henry died a bachelor, without any known offspring in 1751. The reference made to the River Lowther

Introduction

as the pair's 'native stream', and the ensuing descriptions of the village and park of Lowther, affirms that Dalton is actually addressing two of the daughters of Sir Henry's cousin, Robert, the husband of Katherine Lowther.[64] The couple, as mentioned above, had three daughters: Margaret, Katherine, and Barbara. Each of these young ladies knew Dalton, and each could have accompanied him on this excursion.

In addition to praising these two young ladies, Dalton's poem pays its respects to the whole of the Lowther family, and it singles out specific family members for special tribute. Foremost among these is Dalton's patroness, Katherine Lowther, whose virtues figure centrally in the description of the 'home' place with which the poem concludes:

> Her bright example pleas'd to trace,
> Learn every virtue every grace,
> Which lustre give in female life
> To daughter, sister, parent, wife;
> Grateful to see her guardian care
> A tender father's loss repair,
> And, rising far o'er grief and pain,
> The glories of her race maintain.[65]

These lines portray Katherine as a noble matriarch, dutifully fulfilling the role of the late Henry Lowther: the Lord for whose 'return' the 'hopeless tenants' of the estates are said to 'mourn' in the succeeding lines.[66] As the poem closes, Dalton leaves us with a further assertion of Katherine's goodness, and he applauds her commitment to offering aid and providing for the general weal:

> From Lowther She distains to run
> To bask beneath a southern sun,
> Opens the hospitable door,

From the Mines to the Mountains

Fig.5. Detail from A Plan of the Town & Harbour of Whitehaven, *by J. Howard (1811)*

Introduction

> Welcomes the friend, relieves the poor,
> Bides tenants share the lib'ral board,
> And early know and love their lord
> Whose courteous deeds to all extend,
> And make each happy guest a friend.⁶⁷

This depiction of the virtues of the home kept by Katherine is analogically linked in the poem to the celebration of the commercial virtues that had helped Whitehaven to prosper. In both cases, one finds Dalton appealing to an ideal common in much eighteenth-century art and literature: namely, that under the guidance of the benevolent patriarch (or matriarch, as the case may be) the well-ordered estate, town, and nation will flourish.

The Context: Cumberland & Westmorland in Dalton's Era

Having introduced Dalton and his *Descriptive Poem*, it remains for us to survey the scenes his poem portrays. With this task in mind, permit us to follow Dalton into the hills above Whitehaven to consider the town as it appeared during the 1750s. Specifically, we wish to wander up Queen Street to High Street, the eastern edge of the Georgian town (Figure 5), to a building that exemplifies Whitehaven's prosperity in this period: St James' Church.

A View of Georgian Whitehaven

St James' Church was built on a plot of ground granted to the town by Sir James Lowther, and it was consecrated by the Bishop of Carlisle, Richard Osbaldeston (1691–1764), on St James's Day,⁵⁹ July 1753.⁶⁸ (The decision to dedicate the church to Sir James's apostolic namesake was, one suspects, not accidental.) Constructed on a rectilinear plan, St James' is a solid block of a building, and it is well-lit with large, rectangular windows in the sides and Venetian windows in the apse. Neat, but not ostentatious, the church's style seems almost domestic (a large house of God), save for its square tower and double-pedimented entrance. The cost of raising this impressive building was met by subscription, with 107 men and women contributing a total of £2690 to pay for the best pews.[69] To this considerable sum, Sir James added a further donation of £500.

The identity of St James's architect is a matter of some uncertainty. The available evidence suggests that the church's design was produced by Christopher Myers (c. 1717–1789) and/or Carlisle Spedding, the latter of whom (as noted above) was also the steward of the Whitehaven collieries at this time.[70] A year earlier, in July 1752, this ingenious and energetic man wrote that all his spare time was 'employed about building a new church to be called St James'.[71] The first vicar of St James' was to be Spedding's son, Thomas (c.1722–1783), who had been educated to the cloth at Trinity College, Dublin, at the expense of Sir James, who was Thomas's godfather.[72]

Pesvner's guide describes the interior of St James' as 'serenely beautiful', and this praise is not misplaced. Upon entering the church, one steps into a grand vestibule reminiscent of a Georgian mansion. This entryway is flanked by two flights of stairs, which sweep upwards to the galleries on either side of the two large doors that lead into the body of the building. Beyond those doors, one advances into a wide, well-ordered space once commanded from the apse by an ornate three-decker pulpit set almost gallery-high on fluted pilasters (Figure 6).[73] Pennant, during his visit to Whitehaven in 1772, singled out St James' as the Anglican church most worthy of the traveller's attention. He noted that the building was 'elegantly fitted up' with 'a handsome gallery . . . supported by [the] most beautiful ranges of pillars.'[74]

The trustees who oversaw the financing of St James' invested

Introduction

Fig. 6. Interior of St James' Church, Whitehaven

significant funds to beautify the interior of the building. They contracted artists and artisans from near and far, including Dalton's younger brother, Richard (c.1715–1791), who was paid 42 shillings to paint the church's altar during the summer of 1754.[75] In the ceiling above the nave are two stucco roundels attributed to the Irish stuccodore, Robert West, who was paid nearly £24 (a sum equivalent to roughly £2,800 today) for his work.[76] Though now accented by a background of Wedgwood blue, these ornamental fixtures would have once appeared like floating clouds above the congregation (Figure 7).[77] One of these roundels contains a depiction of the Annunciation, the moment of divine conception;

Fig. 6. One of the roundels in St James' Church, Whitehaven.

the other, the one nearest to the altar, depicts the Ascension, the moment of Christ's triumph. To the modern visitor, these two ornaments seem symbols of Georgian Whitehaven itself; they call

Introduction

to mind both the town's humble origins and its remarkable rise.

In 1687/8, Thomas Denton, a one-time London lawyer, undertook a survey of Cumberland for Sir James Lowther's uncle, Sir John Lowther, 1st Viscount Lonsdale (1655–1700) – then the head of the Lowther family. Denton's report includes a description of Whitehaven that emphasises the profits yielded by the Lowthers' investments. The 'buildings' of the town, explains Denton:

> are much enlarged & augmented by the great encrease of trade within this twenty years; the houses being build [sic] of pure white stones, hewen out of the said rock, & the town running along the shore in a figure like an halfe moon, between the cliffe and Branstee-brow. The vessels there are fraught with cole from Hensingham and Morisby pitts, and with salt from Branstee pans and Workington Park, and with grindstones from Whitehaven & St Bees cliffs; and (of late) the merchants have had a corn trade for oats & bigge [barley] principally, in lieu of which commodities, they import French wines and brandee from Burdeux & Naunts; firr, dales [lumber], pitch, tar & cordage from Denmark & Norwey; tobacco & sugar canes from the West Indies.[78]

A contemporaneous painting by the Dutch artist Jan Wyck (1652–1702) provides a complementary portrayal of this small but busy port (Figure 8). Here, half a dozen sea-going vessels ride behind the sheltering harbour wall, known today as the Old Quay. The sandy shore, threaded by Pow Beck, which flows past Market Place, is busy with people carrying burdens, drying sails, lighting fires, and leading goods-laden horses and carts to the waiting vessels. The houses are substantial, three-storey dwellings, facing the shore but backed by several streets. This is the thriving port of Denton's description.

A hundred and twenty years earlier, the local scenery bore a

Fig. 8. Jan Wyck's Harbour of Whitehaven (1686)

rather different appearance. In 1566, the *Calendar of State Papers* recorded only six householders in the locality of Whitehaven.[79] This figure rose to as many as 25 households by 1624, but even then the settlement was hardly renowned as the centre of trade and commerce it would become.[80] In this period, as Nicolson and Burn note, there was 'no shipping save one small pickard of eight or nine ton, at Whitehaven; ... no mariners, except a few fishermen; nothing exported, besides a small quantity of herrings and codfish; nor any thing imported but salt.'[81] It is to this humble village that the 'naked strand' (l. 161) envisioned in Dalton's poem refers.

An engraving purporting to show 'The South East Prospect of

Introduction

Fig. 9. 'The South East Prospect of Whitehaven in the Year 1642'

Whitehaven in the Year 1642' provides a similar depiction of the town in this period. This image, which actually shows a view of Whitehaven from the north east, would appear to have been engraved closer to the date of Dalton's *Descriptive Poem*, and like the poem it offers a retrospective reimagining of the settlement's early history (Figure 9).[82] Here we see the small port where a number of vessels rest beneath the sheltering cliff. There is a straggle of houses along the shore. The chapel of ease stands to the north west of the houses and a rope walk appears to follow the line of what would one day become Senhouse Street. A train of donkeys and packhorses, laden with panniers, are shown carrying their loads to the port.

33

From the Mines to the Mountains

Fig. 10. Matthias Read's A Bird's-Eye View of Whitehaven *(c.1735)*

A contrasting view, taken from near this same point, is provided by Matthias Read (1669–1747). A resident of Whitehaven from the 1690s, Read painted at least half a dozen prospects of the town and harbour.[83] Of these paintings, his *Bird's-Eye View of Whitehaven* (c.1735) is especially noteworthy, both for the depth and boldness of its use of colour and for its topographical particularity (Figure 10). Read presents a neatly delineated panorama of the town, viewed from a point just above the site where thirty years later St James' Church would be built. A windmill and two rope walks running along the line of what was to become George Street frame the lower centre foreground of the picture. To the right are the enclosing arms of the harbour quays. To the left, the Lowther's mansion, Flatt Hall (built by Sir John Lowther between 1676 and 1684), stands solidly in its extensive walled grounds.

Between the mansion and the harbour, the rectilinear network

Introduction

of streets is arranged about the rectangular grounds of St Nicholas' Church. These streets, many of which were named in honour of the monarchy and the aristocracy (hence, King Street, Queen Street, Duke Street, George Street, James Street, and Lowther Street) form part of the 'grid-iron' layout of the eighteenth-century town. The streets beyond Roper Street are shown running slightly out of the true line of this grid, but the only conspicuous irregularity is the clutter of streets in the old port, which is obscured by the shadow of the clouds.

In 1753, looking down from St James' on High Street, you would have gazed upon a prosperous town, not unlike the one portrayed by Dalton, in his poem, and Read, in his painting. This was a new town, a planned town – one of the first in England since the Middle Ages – and it was chiefly the achievement of the vision and ambition of succeeding generations of a single family: the Lowthers.

The Lowthers & Whitehaven

Sir John Lowther (1582–1637) purchased the manor of St Bees in 1630 for the sum of £2,450.[84] Shortly thereafter, he settled his second son, Christopher Lowther (1611–1644), on this newly acquired estate. As J. V. Beckett has observed, Sir John's decision to appoint Christopher as his steward 'was by no means fortuitous.'[85] Christopher was evidently a business-minded man, and with the support of his merchant uncle Robert Lowther (1595–1655), he succeeded in establishing a profitable trade with Dublin in textiles, timber, beef, salt, coal, and herring.[86] A key development within this context was the construction, in 1634, of an 85-yard-long pier to protect the anchorage along Pow Beck. This project, which Christopher oversaw, marks the first stage of the emergence of Whitehaven's modern harbour.[87] Christopher's investments were not, however, exclusively focussed on the shoreline. A decade later, by which time Christopher had been made 1st Baronet of Whitehaven, two parallel streets, King Street and Chapel Street, had been laid out, providing a foundation around which the settlement would gradually expand.[88]

Sir Christopher Lowther died young, but his son, Sir John Lowther (1642–1706), lived to oversee the expansion of the town. This expansion began 'with gusto' (as Beckett notes) in 1663, when John came of age.[89] During John's lifetime, he spent nearly £11,500 securing control of the local coal-bearing land.[90] At Sir John's death, in 1706, Whitehaven was yielding more than 30,500 tons of coal a year.[91]

Most of Sir John Lowther's life was spent in London, where he pursued his own political interests and those of the county. He supervised his affairs in Whitehaven closely by letter, but he only visited the town seven times before retiring in 1698 to Flatt Hall, where he passed the last eight years of his life. He was (in his own words) happy to 'see with others' eyes'.[92] Much of his business in Whitehaven was conducted by his land stewards Thomas Tickell (c.1623–1692) from 1666 and, then, William Gilpin (1657–1724) from 1693.[93] Even more so than his father, Sir John invested significantly in exploiting the local coal reserves. By 1666, Sir John had expressed a desire to possess all the lands, and thereby the mining rights, within a mile of Whitehaven.[94] Twenty years later, he had secured nearly complete control of the area within a five-mile radius of the town.[95]

The coal on the eastern side of Preston Isle, above Pow Beck, had long been exploited on a small scale through surface adits and small pits worked by freeholder miners. Lowther sought to work the coal in a more systematic fashion. In the 1670s, a level was driven horizontally from Pow Beck to tap and drain the higher, six-foot Bannock Seam, which dipped gently to the west and north. Entry to the seam for men, horses, and materials was by a

Introduction

'bearmouth', which cut directly into the seam where it outcropped on the hillside. As the miners penetrated deeper along the seam, rather than haul the coal out through the bearmouth, shallow shafts were sunk to raise the coal, first by hand windlasses and, in later years, by horse-powered gins. In the 1680s, the nine-foot Main Band was discovered a hundred feet below the Bannock Band at Howgill. It was drained by an underground level and the water pumped to the surface by a horse-powered gin. As the workings penetrated further down along the seam, the operations became more hazardous and drainage became more problematic. New pits were sunk and further levels driven, and water was drained by the cumbersome process of barrels and underground gins.[96]

As the number of pits grew, so too did Whitehaven, and Sir John maintained a self-interested and paternalistic oversight of the town. In 1688, he commissioned Andrew Pellin (d.1732) to draw up a 'true model of [the] towne', and the plan Pellin produced clearly displays the developing grid-iron devised by extending and crossing the lines of King Street and Chapel Street (Figure 11).[86] Lowther Street, the town's new main thoroughfare, was to be sixteen-yards wide and to run from the Lowther's mansion to the harbour.[98] The streets set at right angles from this central axis were to be ten-yards wide. They were, moreover, to be separated by numbered building plots, each of which was to be fifteen feet wide. In addition to promoting the planned development of the town, Sir John made investments 'to draw people hither', by building and providing loans.[99] He helped restore the grammar school at St Bees and promoted a school in Whitehaven, where 'most of the neighbouring gentry have their sons fitted either for the university or merchandize in this town'.[100] In the early 1690s, moreover, he provided the land and a portion of the funds for a new church, St Nicholas'. This impressive building could seat a congregation of 1,100 and, with its spacious precinct, it became a landmark of the

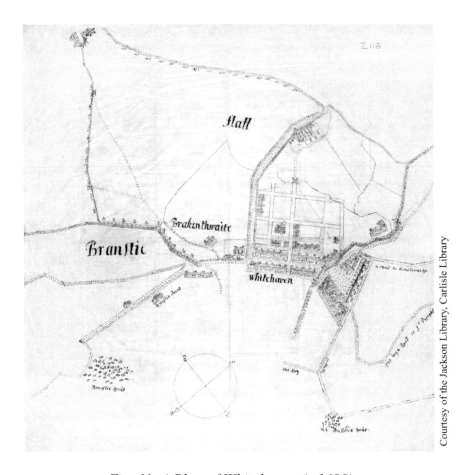

Fig. 11. A Plan of Whitehaven (c.1690)

growing community, which by 1695 had risen to 2,280.[101]

The antiquary Sir Ralph Thoresby (1658–1725), who journeyed through Whitehaven in 1694, provides a concise description of the changes affected by these various investments. 'Whitehaven', writes Thoresby:

is absolutely the most growing thriving town in these parts;

Introduction

much encouraged by Sir John Lowther, the lord thereof, who gave them four hundred pounds towards building the pier, and two hundred pounds towards the building of a church, which is one of the prettiest I have seen, . . . with the ground that it stands upon; and he is now building a very stately schoolhouse, to which he designs the addition of two wings, one for teaching the mathematics, and the other writing.[102]

From a lowly hamlet, Whitehaven had risen to become the very model of a modern English town.

Sir John's second son, Sir James Lowther (1673–1755), inherited this burgeoning town and the commercial enterprise that supported its growth in 1706. In 1731, moreover, Sir James inherited the baronetcy of Whitehaven from his profligate brother, Sir Christopher Lowther (1666–1731). In his turn, Sir James spent over £46,000 protecting and extending his control of much of the west Cumberland coalfield.[103] This determined and ambitious man became, with an annual income of £25,000 a year, reputedly the 'richest commoner in England'.[104] Nicolson and Burn, in their account of Whitehaven in 1777, adjudged that 'the late Sir James Lowther, baronet, by improvement of the coal works, advanced th[e] town to such a degree, that he lived to see about eleven thousand inhabitants, and about two hundred and sixty sail of ships, of near thirty thousand tun burden.'[105] True to this assessment, under Lowther's management, the local pits had trebled their annual output and had yielded a six-fold increase in their profits. In 1708, the Whitehaven collieries produced 34,209 tons; in 1750, their total production had risen to 126,129 tons.[106]

Sir James's methods could be ruthless, but he was seeking to protect and extend the near monopoly of the coal trade which he had inherited from his father. Faced by a depressed market in the early 1720s and the competition from smaller coal owners such as the Curwen and Senhouse families, Lowther determined to strengthen his control by extending his ownership in the west Cumberland coalfield. In 1722, he bought the manors of Ribton and Dearham from Richard Lamplugh for £6,000; four years later, he paid Thomas Patrickson more than £2,252 for Stockhow and John Ponsonby £2,100 for Weddicar.[107] Sir James baulked at paying high prices, but through these strategic acquisitions he established himself as 'the major figure in the coal trade at all four ports along the coast' by the 1740s.[108] By the early 1750s, he may have been responsible for as much as 90% of the coal exported from west Cumberland.[109]

Sir John Clerk of Penicuik, himself a mine owner, visited Whitehaven to appraise the mines in 1739, and was not impressed by Sir James, opining: 'The 3d curiosity at Whitehaven or rather the greatest, is Sr Ja. Louder himself who in the midest of great riches lives but in a poor way. He is an indolent old man and knows nothing about coalworks.'[110] Sir James, according to one traveller fifty years after his death, was 'well known for his extreme penuriousness, which obtained him the appellation of "Farthing Jemmy."'[111] One unsubstantiated anecdote tells of him returning to a London coffee-house because he had been given a bad half-penny.[112]

John Wesley (1703–1791), in a letter to Sir James of 28 October 1754, was very direct in weighing up the man and his values. 'I believe you to be an honest, upright Man', writes Wesley; 'I love you for having protected an innocent People from their cruel and lawless Oppressors. But . . . I fear you are covetous; that you love the World.'[113] Wesley then proceeded to repeat the defence Sir James had offered of his character in a previous letter:

> The Substance of your Answer was, That many People exhort others to Charity, from Self-Interest; That Men of Fortune must mind their Fortune; That you can't go about to look for poor People; That when you have seen them yourself, and relieved

Introduction

them, they were scarce ever satisfied; . . . That you have also given to several Hospitals, an hundred Pounds at a Time; But that you must support your Family; That the Lowther Family has continued above 400 Years; That you are for great Things; for public Charities, and for saving the Nation from Ruin; And that others may think as they please; but this is your Way of thinking, and has been for many Years.[114]

These statements reveal a good deal about Sir James's character. They indicate that he was a man with a strong sense of self and, even though he never married and was without issue, a strong sense of the Lowther family interest and a disdain for the indigent poor. He was a man who felt that his wealth brought its own responsibilities. Another of Sir James's acquaintances regarded him as a man who, after money, 'was desirous of possessing nothing more than the respect, dependence and almost adoration of his friends and relations'.[115] In Whitehaven, according to his own account, he received the adulation and respect he felt he deserved. He once described how he was met 'on the high road by the high sheriff, chief gentlemen, clergymen and principal freeholders living for about thirty miles in length in that part of the country, who accompanied him (to Whitehaven) where he was received by thousands in the high streets, the bells ringing, the great guns firing and the ships putting out their colours.'[116]

The high self-regard registered in these statements was complemented by Sir James's self-discipline and his indomitable determination. Abstemious in his diet and temperate in his habits, Sir James refrained from 'strong drink' from his late twenties onwards.[117] He was, nonetheless, frequently plagued by gout in his later life. In spite of these bouts of illness and, eventually, the amputation of his right leg, Sir James proved resilient in pursuing his commercial and political interests. He became the longest serving Member of Parliament, having sat variously for Carlisle,

Appleby, and Cumberland for over sixty years.

Sir James came to Whitehaven, perhaps, once every two years, to settle matters which could not be settled at a distance, but his business in Whitehaven was in the safe hands of a group of remarkable men: William Gilpin, the lawyer who had served his father, and later the brothers, Carlisle and John Spedding (1685–1758).

The Spedding Brothers

John Spedding was the ideal agent for Sir James in Whitehaven. He had proved himself in the years when he was first taken on as a domestic servant at Flatt Hall, in 1700, at the age of fifteen. Over a period of time, Spedding 'exposed [the] double-dealing and embezzlement' of Lowther's mining agent, John Gale (d.1716).[118] Spedding was a doggedly trustworthy man, whose thrice-weekly correspondence with Sir James, reveals someone who was, according to J. D. Marshall:

> somewhat obsessed with the complexities of his task, slow to make up his mind and rather a worrier. His letters are exercises in "thinking aloud", full of second thoughts and packed with long, barely punctuated tracts of near-labyrinthine speculation regarding the working of the colliery, faithfully reporting every incident of note and purveying every rumour that might be of use to his master.[119]

In such a capacity, John served Sir James for sixty years until his death. During that time, as he was able to tell Sir James, 'The improvement of your estate has been the chief concern of my life.'[120] From the time he succeeded William Gilpin as land agent in 1728, he was not particularly well remunerated, but Sir James ensured he retained John's loyalty by supporting his private ventures in (amongst other things) timber, shipping, and brewing and by showing a concern for the Spedding family.

In the same way, John's younger brother, Carlisle was Sir James's right hand man in everything else to do with the mines. In 1716, Carlisle's salary was only £17 a year. This sum was raised to £25 in 1720 and then to £35 in 1721, when there was a possibility that he might leave to work for Thomas Newcomen (1664–1729) on his new steam engine. From 1730, when Carlisle succeeded his brother as colliery steward, he was paid £50 per annum. (Significantly, though, after Sir James's death, Spedding's salary was increased to £150.[121]) For this relatively meagre outlay, Sir James received the services of a man who, in Marshall's estimation, should be 'regarded as one of the great mining engineers'.[122] Sir James originally took Carlisle on when the career prospects of this fourth son of an impoverished tenant seemed bleak.[123] He had been expected 'to put to sea with some of John Gale's sons', but following Gale's dismissal John Spedding persuaded Sir James to permit his brother 'to assist about the business of the collieries'.[124] Carlisle, as he proved himself and demonstrated his engineering abilities, found his responsibilities increasing.

Carlisle first proved his remarkable engineering aptitude in 1716, when it was decided to install the predecessor of the fire-engines, whose prodigious power Dr Brownrigg details in his notes to Dalton's poem. The old system of removing the water with horse-powered cog-and-rung gins was cumbersome and expensive; the cost made mining uneconomical long before the coal seams were exhausted. Thomas Savery (c.1650–1715) had invented and patented a steam engine for pumping water in 1698, and this machine had been used in London for a few water supplies. In the autumn of 1712, however, Sir James saw a demonstration of a new type of engine, which had been developed by Thomas Newcomen.

Newcomen's beam engine could raise more water more efficiently and to a greater height. Its use would enable new mines to be dug ever deeper. In 1716, Whitehaven's first Newcomen engine (the sixth in the country) was installed at the Stone Pit by Carlisle Spedding and Newcomen's assistant, John Calley (1663–1717), to raise water from the Main Band so that it could be channelled out through the drainage level to the Bannock Band. The housing for the machine cost more than £85 and 76 feet of timber was required for 'the Large Beames' which operated the pump.[125] The antiquarian William Stukeley, who passed through Whitehaven in 1725, was as much taken as John Dalton with the operation of the pump:

> At last the famous fire-engine discharges the water, which is a notable piece of machinery working itself intirely [sic]: it creates a vacuum by first rarifying [sic] the air with hot steam, then condenses it suddenly by cold water; whence a piston is drawn up and down alternately, at one end of a beam: this actuates a pump at the other end, which, let down into the works, draws the water out: it makes about 14 strokes in a minute; so that it empties 140 hogsheads in an hour, with moderate working.[126]

It was thus Thomas Newcomen rather than the 'Sagacious Savery' celebrated in Dalton's poem (l.135) who deserved credit for the effective engine.

    The successful expansion of Whitehaven's mines was dependent on such technological advances. There were seven seams of coal varying in thickness from two to nine feet, which dipped at a declination of between 1:5 and 1:8 to the west under the sea. Landslips had produced what the miners called dykes where the level of the seam was broken. The seams were often waterlogged and there were frequent pockets of explosive firedamp (methane or hydrogen sulphide) and asphyxiating choke damp (carbon dioxide). The scale on which the Lowther collieries

Introduction

operated required great efficiency, not only in the sinking of the pits and the excavation of the coal, but also in the delivery of the coal to ships. In all these matters, Carlisle Spedding's developing practical and technical expertise was to prove invaluable.

In 1729, at the age of thirty-four, Carlisle was about to begin sinking the pit at Saltom.[127] This task was, as his brother reflected, 'a great undertaking' – 'perhaps the boldest thing that ever was undertaken'– and it would make serious demands of Carlisle's skills and ingenuity.[128] The mine was to be sunk on the western side of Preston Isle to the unprecedented depth of eighty fathoms (480 ft). An area was cleared within twenty yards of the highwater mark above Saltom Bay and the resulting platform was protected by a sea wall. The shaft was an eight-by-ten-foot oval, which enabled it to be partitioned with one section being available to draw coal and the other drawing water by means of the Newcomen fire-engine which was being installed on the surface at a cost of over £100. A horse-gin was constructed to raise the coal. The divided shaft system would have assisted with ventilation and it may have been the beginning of the more sophisticated forms of ventilation by 'coursing the air' which Spedding later developed.[129]

At a depth of 42 fathoms, the miners encountered a serious problem when they struck a pocket of firedamp. The difficulties were reported to the Royal Society in London by James Lowther, but the paper he presented certainly owed much to Spedding's first-hand experiences. (Indeed, the paper may have even been written by Spedding himself.) This paper, 'An Account of the Damp Air in a Coal-Pit', described the problems caused by firedamp and indicated something of the casual way in which miners dealt with this often-fatal hazard:

> When the Workmen first prick'd the Black-Stone Bed, which was on the rise Side of the Pit, it afforded very little Water, contrary to what was expected; but instead thereof a vast

Quantity of damp corrupted Air, which bubbled through a Quantity of Water, then spread over that part of the Pit, and made a great hissing Noise; at which the Workmen being somewhat surpriz'd, held a Candle towards it, and it immediately took Fire on the Surface of the Water, and burned very fiercely; the Flame being about half a Yard in Diameter, and near two Yards high, which frightened the Workmen, so that they took the Rope, and went up the Pit, having first extinguished the Flame, by beating it out with their Hats[.][130]

After these events, Spedding seems to have gone down to investigate the situation accompanied by one of the miners. They lit the gas and watched it burn for half an hour till it covered the bottom of the pit:

> They then extinguished the Flame as before, and opened the Black-Stone Bed near two Foot broad, that a greater Quantity of Air might issue forth, and then fired it again; it burn'd a full Yard in Diameter, and about three Yards high, which soon heated the Pit to so great a Degree, that the Men were in Danger of being stifled, and so were as expeditious as possible in extinguishing the Flame, which was then too strong to be beaten out with their Hats; but with the Assistance of a Spout of Water, of four Inches Diameter, let down from a Cistern above, they happily got it extinguished without further Harm.[131]

The shaft was sunk further, the area partitioned off, and a two-inch square leather pipe was installed to conduct the 'damp air' to the surface. Three years later, they collected a sample of the air in a bladder. Sir James demonstrated to the Royal Society how, when the air was released, it could be lit by a candle and would continue to burn until the bladder was exhausted.[132] The findings reported in the paper also had practical applications. Specifically, the

Introduction

observation that 'damp Air, will not take Fire except by Flame; Sparks do not affect it,' informed the invention of the Spedding mill.[133]

Spedding was also responsible for devising the intricate system of ventilation in the mines. This network of pipes, shafts, and vents was described by Henry Hobhouse during his tour of the North in 1774. 'These mines', write Hobhouse, 'are often troubled with damps or foul air, to prevent the consequences of which they have many shafts. Over the shafts they build a chimney like a round acute cone once upon top, & under it they raise a fire which by experience they find to contribute much to purify & discharge the air; & below they have frequent doors to direct the course & communication of the air.'[134] James Eyre Weeks, in his 'Poetical Prospect of Whitehaven' (1752), found Spedding's work to be worthy of poetic description:

> Near are the coalworks, Lowther's treasur'd mines,
> Whence the foul-air, thro' artful tube refines,
> Like a Volcano the perennial Flame
> Sulphureous burns in nature much the same,
> Yet so by art contriv'd that thro' the fire,
> The pestilential vapour may transpire,
> The air expurg'd above, and free to breathe,
> Th' adventrous collier works insur'd beneath.[135]

Two years after the work on Saltom Pit began, on 9 February 1731, the first coals were drawn from the mine. The expenditure had been in excess of £1,900.[136] Further work on the quay built on the exposed Saltom head and on engine repairs and replacements, and other matters over the following year, resulted in a final bill of more than £4,520.[137] Salt pans were constructed at the pit head to make efficient use of excess coal. The dedicated quay, built on the headland, in part to avoid harbour dues in Whitehaven, was battered and damaged by storms, and proved impracticable. However, this bold enterprise, which required remarkable commercial courage and entrepreneurship, as well as engineering skills of the highest order, resulted in the production of 270,000 tons of coal by 1751.[138]

With the Saltom quay unusable, the coal had to be raised by horse gin through the Ravenhead Pit to the top of the cliff. This coal was delivered to the quay at Whitehaven by another of Carlisle Spedding's cost-saving innovations: a 'gravity wagonway'.[139] Some fifty years later, Joshua Dixon (1743-1825), still thought the wagonway sufficiently remarkable to enthusiastically describe it in detail:

> The coals are conveyed to the ships by a very ingenious contrivance which was first practiced by Mr Carlisle Spedding. Frames of wood are placed, in an exactly parallel line, along the road, leading from the pits. . . . The loaden [sic] waggon is carried upon these frames down the inclined plane, not by the labour of horses, or of men, but according to a simple law in mechanics, by its own weight. The occasional assistance of one man is necessary, to prevent the waggon from acquiring too great a velocity, in consequence of a quick descent in the road. This is performed by two levers, connected with the first pair of wheels: the friction of which regulates their motion: and as the power is applied at a distance, an inconsiderable exertion is sufficient for the purpose. . . . [T]he waggons proceed in this manner, until they arrive at a covered gallery made of wood, which is elevated about 37 feet above the level of the quay. From this gallery, the necessary supply of coals is obtained, by means of spouts. Five of these are fixed, at an angle of about 45 degrees; and so conveniently distant from each other, as that 5 vessels, of very considerable burthen may be loaded, at one tide, under them. The bottom of the waggon being opened, the coals run, with great rapidity, down the spout into the ship. When there are no vessels ready to receive the

coals, they are dropped, through holes, left in the gallery, into the magazine; the bottom of which is about 25 feet below the gallery, or waggon way.[140]

James Weeks, in his 'Poetical Prospect of Whitehaven', also remarked on the wonder of Spedding's 'ingenious contrivance'. In terms not unlike those employed in Dalton's *Descriptive Poem*, Weeks portrayed Spedding as being something of a magician:

> Lo! here a lifeless waggon at thy will,
> True to its ambit, circles round a hill,
> Down the descent by Spedding's wond'rous art,
> The waggon-way retains the flying cart.
> So far from being cumber'd with its freight,
> Like virtue———see it grows beneath a weight,
> Down plains inclin'd the self-mov'd engines fly
> To load the Ships which near the Hurry's lie.
> Thro' wooden spouts descends the sooty ore,
> An export grateful to Hibernias shore.[141]

Magician or not, Spedding was evidently a courageous man, and his bravery was amply demonstrated during an explosion at the Corporal Pit in August 1737. Twenty-three men were killed by the explosion. Spedding led the rescue brigade and 'saved the life of one man with great hazard of his own.'[142] Despite the damage it did to his health, he insisted on exposing himself to the dangers of the mines. As his brother John explained in a letter to Sir James following the explosion:

> I have told him over and over that you do not expect he should run such risks . . . [but Carlisle] says if he had not been there and were not always with [the men] upon such occasions they are so miskillful [sic] or foolhardy that many more of them would have been destroyed, and he cannot keep back, though

he know it is destruction to his health to be long in the bad air.[143]

Dr Brownrigg, who treated Carlisle during his illness, described how 'in the summer last past [when Spedding had] entered mines full of stifling gases, his strength scarcely sufficed to see the light of day again, from that time he complained of headache and frequent throbbing of the cephalic arteries, and when he concentrated of failure of internal senses'.[144] Later, when miners refused to return to work in the pits, Spedding accompanied by his son, had to take the lead in order to prove they were safe.

The pits were dangerous places. Visitors to the Saltom pit, including the two ladies described in Dalton's poem, entered that vast chamber beneath the sea perhaps little aware of how treacherous it could be. Weeks, in another poem celebrating the commercial energy of west Cumberland, 'A Poetical Prospect of the Coast, Town, and Harbour of Workington', evinced some sympathy for the miners' conditions and showed some apprehension of the dangers thy faced:

> There down the Pits descend the human moles,
> And pick the Passage thro' the Veiny Coals,
> Maintain thro' ev'ry obstacle their Way,
> And force their entrance ev'n beneath the Sea,
> All as their dangr'ous Conquests they Extend,
> The Works with mighty Pillars they defend,
> To prop the pondrous Roof that hangs above,
> Which threatens Ravage to their deep Alcove;
> Tremendous crush! How dreadfully they die,
> Then ill supported, tumbling from on high,
> Upon their heads the heavy Ruins lye![145]

Carlisle Spedding, the 'Prospero' of the mines, knew of the dangers of these working conditions all too well. He was killed by

Introduction

an explosion on 8 August 1755. His loyal brother, John, survived him by just three years.

Dr William Brownrigg (1711–1800)

The Dr Brownrigg who treated Spedding in 1737 was the same man who supplied the notes to Dalton's *Descriptive Poem*. Brownrigg had been born at High Close Hall, near Aspatria, the son of a landowner. Apprenticed to John Atkinson, a Carlisle surgeon and apothecary, he studied medicine in London for two years between 1733 and 1735. In 1736, he graduated MD from Leiden, then one of the leading medical schools in Europe, where he studied under Herman Boerhaave.[146] Boerhaave was a pioneer of clinical and quantitative medicine and Brownrigg's meticulous report on Spedding's treatment illustrates how he put Boerhaave's methods into practice. Brownrigg's thesis, *De praxi medica ineunda* (1737), demonstrated the commitment to advanced medical practice that he brought to his work in Whitehaven.

Brownrigg came to Whitehaven to practise as a physician and apothecary alongside Richard Senhouse (d.1737), who had also been a student in Leiden. Senhouse died shortly after Brownrigg's arrival, though, and Brownrigg, who lived at 24 Queen Street, was consequently able to develop a county-wide medical practice, attending to patients both in his consulting rooms in Whitehaven and as far afield as Carlisle in the north and Millom in the south. In 1741, he married John Spedding's daughter Mary (1721–1794), and, in many ways, he spent his next years working alongside the Speddings, being concerned with the mines and mining practice, involving himself with the health and well-being of the town, and developing business interests of his own.

Brownrigg acted as Sir James Lowther's personal physician when he was in Whitehaven, and, in 1743, Sir James gave money towards the building of a laboratory, where Carlisle Spedding had arranged for a piped supply of firedamp.[147] After the explosion in 1737 and the considerable loss of life, Brownrigg made the investigation of firedamp one of his prime concerns. Through Lowther's agency, he submitted five papers on firedamp to the Royal Society, noting the relation of the gas to epidemics, mineral waters, and the nature of common air, as well as the possibility of being able to predict explosions according to barometric pressure.[148]

As early as 1741, Brownrigg suggested to Sir Hans Sloane (1660–1753), then President of the Royal Society, that 'I may probably sometime or other digest my observations into a History of Coal Mines'.[149] (This is the history he mentions in the letter appended at the conclusion of Dalton's *Descriptive Poem*.) An outline of the history was read to the Royal Society in 1756, but the work itself was never completed. Brownrigg was made a member of the Society in 1742, and, in 1766, after submitting a paper on spa water, which contained many of his earlier observations on gases escaping from mineral waters, he was awarded the Society's Copley Medal. Scientific work and technological innovation were proceeding alongside commercial development. The nature of air and gases was little understood at the time. This paper and earlier (thitherto unpublished) papers from the 1740s on firedamp and choke-damp were to prove useful to Henry Cavendish in his later work on the gases.[150] In 1748, moreover, Brownrigg published an important booklet on *The Art of Making Common Salt*. This work was representative of the breadth of his interests and concerns; it looked to contribute to improving the health of the nation and providing work in the fisheries as well as furthering the technology and science of the subject.

In 1760, Brownrigg retired to the estate he inherited at Ormathwaite on the southern slopes of Skiddaw. He continued with his scientific work there, building a laboratory and sending papers on epidemiology and salts to the Royal Society. By this time, he

Introduction

had acquired considerable business interests as well, including a rope manufactory in Whitehaven. In 1765, Brownrigg partnered with Anthony Bacon and Charles Wood in developing the Cyfarthfa Ironworks in South Wales. He also involved himself with agriculture and forestry (he had leased Skiddaw Forest in 1750 with the intention of exploiting the timber). He acquired a very fine collection of paintings and he received many guests.

The long list of visitors who called on Brownrigg at Ormathwaite offers an indication of the esteem in which he was held – both locally and nationally. Notably, many of the earlier travellers and celebrants of the mountains and lakes of Cumberland and Westmorland benefitted from his hospitality and his expert knowledge. The poet Thomas Gray (1716–1771) visited Brownrigg while touring the region in 1769; the cleric and aesthete William Gilpin stayed with Brownrigg in 1772 while compiling his *Observations Relative Chiefly to Picturesque Beauty* (1786); and the priest and antiquary Thomas West, author of the first *Guide to the Lakes*, was also a visitor in the 1770s. Benjamin Franklin and Sir John Pringle (1707–1782), then President of the Royal Society, were Brownrigg's guests in 1772, when they conducted a famous experiment by pouring a little oil on the troubled waters of Derwentwater.[151] Franklin, who was 65 at the time, left little record of his time with Brownrigg. In a letter home to his wife Dorothy, though, he mentioned briefly his ascent of a high fell (presumably Skiddaw) and his descent beneath the sea in the collieries at Whitehaven:

> In Cumberland I ascended a very high Mountain, where I had a prospect of a most beautiful Country, of Hills, Fields, Lakes, Villa's, &c., and at Whitehaven went down the Coal-mines till they told me I was 80 fathoms under the Surface of the Sea, which roll'd over our Heads; so that I have been nearer both the upper and lower Regions than ever in my Life before.[152]

From the Mines to the Mountains

This tour of the mines and mountains had become conventional by this period. Several contemporaneous travellers made a point of visiting both during their time in Cumberland.[153]

Franklin was probably escorted in the Saltom colliery by James Spedding (1720–1788), Carlisle's son and successor. Even though Franklin made only a brief mention of the mines, the visit proved important to him. Six months later he mentioned his journey in a letter to the French botanist and physician, Jacques Barbeu-Dubourg (1709–1779). Franklin had been closely observant of the fossils in the roof of the mine and this led him to think of the possibility of stratification and earth movements. The investigation of geology was at an early stage and the journey into the pits represented an opportunity to investigate and speculate on the structure of the rocks. Franklin sought to draw scientific conclusions from his observations:

> I am persuaded as well as you, that the Sea Coal has a vegetable origin, and that it has been formed near the surface of the earth; but as preceding convulsions of nature had served to bury it very deep in many places, and covered with many different strata, we are indebted to subsequent convulsions for having brought within our view the extremities of its veins, so as to lead us to penetrate the earth in search of it. I visited last summer a large coal-mine at Whitehaven in Cumberland; and in following the vein, and descending by degrees towards the sea, I penetrated below the ocean, where the level of its surface was more than [80] fathom above my head; and the miners assured me that their works extended some miles beyond the place where I then was, continually and gradually descending under the sea. The slate which forms the roof of this coal-mine is impressed in many places with the figures of leaves and branches of fern, which undoubtedly grew at the surface, when the slate was in the state of sand on the banks of the sea. Thus it appears

Introduction

that this vein of coal has suffered a prodigious settlement.[115]

The impressions he had taken from Whitehaven were still in his mind when, ten years later, writing to the French geologist, Jean-Louis Giraud Soulavie (1751–1813), he observed:

I did not find Coal mines under the Calcareous rock in Derbyshire. I only remarked that at the lowest Part of that rocky Mountain which was in sight, there were Oyster Shells mixed with the Stone; & part of the high County of Derby being probably as much above the level of the Sea, as the Coal Mines of Whitehaven were below, it seemed a proof that there had been a great Bouleversement in the Surface of that Island some part of it having been depressed under the Sea, & other Parts which had been under it being raised above it. Such Changes in the superficial Parts of the Globe seemed to me unlikely to happen if the Earth were solid to the Center. I therefore imagined that the internal parts might be a fluid more dense, & of greater specific gravity than any of the Solids we are acquainted with; which therefore might swim in or upon that Fluid. Thus the surface of the Globe would be a Shell, capable of being broken & disordered by the violent movements of the fluid on which it rested.[155]

Two weeks prior to Franklin's visit, Brownrigg had hosted another fellow of the Royal Society: Thomas Pennant. Like Brownrigg, he was a man of wide and diverse interests. His particular concern was natural history. He corresponded with Carl Linnaeus, the great Swedish taxonomist, and with Gilbert White in Selborne. Before setting out on his travels, Pennant had contacted local authorities, such as Brownrigg, in the areas he intended to visit. He was far from being a casual tourist and his visit to Whitehaven will have been undertaken with the intention of making a proper survey of the town, port, and mines. He was also interested in history and antiquities and a keen observer of the agriculture, as well as plant and animal life.

On 25 May 1772, Pennant, Brownrigg and their party left Ormathwaite and made their way through Cockermouth and Distington ('a long and dirty town') until they approached Whitehaven. His commentary on the town, from which we have quoted above, is worth reproducing here at length as a pendant to the foregoing account:

> The town is in a manner a new creation. . . . The rise of the place is owing to the collieries, improved and encouraged by the family of the Lowthers, to their great emolument. . . . At this time the town may boast of being one of the handsomest in the north of England, built of stone, and the streets pointing strait to the harbour, with others crossing them at right angles. It is as populous as it is elegant, containing twelve thousand inhabitants, and has a hundred and ninety great ships belonging to it, mostly employed in the coal trade.
>
> The tobacco trade is much declined: formerly about twenty thousand hogsheads were annually imported from Virginia, now scarce a fourth of that number; Glasgow having stolen that branch: but to make amends, another is carried on to the West-Indies, where hats, printed linens, hams, &c. are sent. . . The improvements in the adjacent lands keep pace with those in the town: the Brainsty estate forty years ago was set for as many pounds; at present, by dint of good husbandry, especially liming, is encreased to five hundred and seventy-one. . . .
>
> The harbour is artificial, but a fine and expensive work, on the south end, guarded by a long pier, where the ships may lie in great security. Another is placed farther out, to break the force of the sea; and within these are two long strait tongues, or quays, where the vessels are lodged: close to the shore, on the south side, is another, covered with what is called here a Steer, having in the lower part a range of smiths shops, and

Introduction

above an extensive floor, capable of containing six thousand waggon loads of coal, of 4200 lb. each. But this is only used as a sort of magazine: for above this are covered galleries with rail roads, terminating in large flues, or hurries, placed sloping over the quay, and thro' these the coal is discharged out of the waggons into the holds of the ships, rattling down with a noise like thunder. Commonly eight ships, from a hundred and twenty to a hundred tuns each, have been loaden in one tide; and on extraordinary occasions twelve. Each load is put on board for ten shillings: and the waggons, after being emptied, are brought round into the road by a turn frame, and drawn back by a single horse. The greater part of the way from the pits, which lie about three or four miles distant from the hurries is down hill; the waggon is steered by one man, with a sort of rudder to direct it; so that he can retard or accelerate the motion by the pressure he gives by it on the wheel.

Many other works are projected to secure the port, particularly another pier on the north side, which when complete, will render this haven quite land-locked. It is to be observed, that in coming in vessels should carry a full sail till they pass the pier head, otherwise they will not be carried far enough in. The greatest part of the coal is sent to Ireland, where about two hundred and eighteen thousand tons are annually exported.[156]

After noting the elegance of the town, and the bustle and industry of the harbour, Pennant and his party were escorted through the mines by James Spedding on a journey not unlike the one described in Dalton's *Descriptive Poem*. Pennant seems to adopt the miners' sense that the danger of firedamp had been 'almost overcome' by the system of boarding and ventilation. He mentions that the gas was not being burnt off at the flues above the mine. He does, however, note that there are still areas where it is dangerous to have a lighted candle. It is possible that the miners still worked mostly by the light of candles and used a Spedding mill, which required one man to turn it constantly, only in the areas of the mine affected by firedamp:

> Visit the collieries, entering at the foot of a hill, not distant from the town, attended by the agent: the entrance was a narrow passage, bricked and vaulted, sloping down with an easy descent. Reach the first beds of coal which had been worked about a century ago: the roofs are smooth and spacious, the pillars of sufficient strength to support the great superstructure, being fifteen yards square, or sixty in circumference; not above a third of the coal having been worked in this place; so that to me the very columns seemed left as resources for fuel in future times. The immense caverns that lay between the pillars, exhibited a most gloomy appearance: I could not help enquiring here after the imaginary inhabitant, the creation of the laborers fancy,
>
> The swart Fairy of the mine.[157]
>
> and was seriously answered by a black fellow at my elbow, that he really had never met with any; but that his grandfather had found the little implements and tools belonging to this diminutive race of subterraneous spirits.[158]
>
> The beds of coal are nine or ten feet thick: and dip to the west one yard in eight. In various parts are great bars of stone, which cut off the coal: if they bend one way, they influence the coal to rise above one's head; if another, to sink beneath the feet. Operations of nature past my skill to unfold.
>
> Reach a place where there is a very deep descent; the colliers call this Hardknot, from the mountain of that name; and another Wrynose. At about eighty fathoms depth began to see the workings of the rods of the fire-engine, and the present operations of the colliers, who work now in security, for the

Introduction

fire-damps, formerly so dangerous, are almost overcome; at present they are prevented by boarded partitions, placed a foot distant from the sides, which causes a free circulation of air throughout: but as still there are some places not capable of such conveniencies, the colliers, who dare not venture with a candle in spots where fire-damps are supposed to lurk, have invented a curious machine to serve the purpose of lights: it is what they call a steel-mill, consisting of a small wheel and a handle; this they turn with vast rapidity against a flint, and the great quantity of sparks emitted, not only serves for a candle, but has been found of such a nature as not to set fire to the horrid vapour.

Formerly the damp or fiery vapour was conveyed thro' pipes to the open air, and formed a terrible illumination during night, like the eruptions of a volcano; and by its heat water could be boiled: the men who worked in it inhaled inflammable air, and if they breathed against a candle, puffed out a fiery stream; so that I make no doubt, was the experiment made, the same phænomenon would appear as John Grub attributed to my illustrious countryman Pendragon, chief of Britons.[159]

Reached the extremity of this black journey to a place near two miles from the entrance, beneath the sea, where probably ships were then sailing over us. Returned up the laborious ascent, and was happy once more to emerge into day-light.[160]

'Sweet Keswick's Vale'

During the two days Thomas Pennant spent with William Brownrigg at Ormathwaite, he used his time to the full: Brownrigg showed him Castlerigg Stone Circle; they sailed round Derwentwater, noting its greatest depth of twenty feet and observing the local mines and the salt springs; they climbed Skiddaw and explored the 'Alpine scenery' of the area; and they found time to discuss topics ranging from the local agriculture and economy to folk-lore and etymology. They also examined Brownrigg's collection of antiquities and minerals. Pennant was much taken with the 'great variety of the ores of Borrowdale, such as lead, common and fibrous, black-jack, and black-lead or wad'.[161]

The Black Lead mine and mining for other non-ferrous metals and slate-quarrying had long been an important part of the Borrowdale economy. The Company of The Mines Royal, led by a German miner, Daniel Hoechstetter from Augsburg, had been established in 1565.[162] The black-lead was essential to Britain's military prowess. This pure form of graphite was so invaluable for the casting of bombs and cannon balls and the cleaning of arms, that, in 1751, a dedicated Act of Parliament had made stealing black wadd from the mine at Seathwaite, in Borrowdale, a felony punishable by a year's hard labour and public whipping.[163] It was also useful in the lining of crucibles for the fusing of metals and the glazing of earthenware, and for the making of pencils. George Smith of Wigton visited the mines in the late 1740s. After riding the ten miles from Keswick, he was confronted with a 'frightful' scene, where the 'precipices were surprisingly variegated with spices, prominencies [sic], spouting jets of water, cataracts, and rivers that were precipitated from the cliffs with an alarming noise'.[164] He saw eighteen people digging with mattocks in the spoil heaps of the black wadd mine: 'these fellows', he reports, 'could generally clear 6 or 8 shillings a day, and sometimes more.'[165]

When Smith, who knew the fells extremely well, looked across the 'large plain to the West' above the mine he felt he was at the ends of the earth. Thomas Pennant, perhaps, looking from the vantage point of Ormathwaite had shared this view. For him, 'the fells of Borrowdale' seemed to 'frown . . . like a hardened tyrant.'[166] Others offered a very different view of Borrowdale. William

Introduction

Camden (1551–1623) had been charmed by the scene, and a century later Thomas Denton reported on a 'Borodale' that was then 'an inclusive mannor [sic] of Sir Wilfrid Lawson'. Denton saw a pastoral and productive landscape, where 'The inhabitants are enriched by their great stocks of sheep, which with a little charge do greatly increase their numbers and their owners' wealth.'[167] It was the same beneficent landscape which Thomas Cowper, the curate of Loweswater, described in his *Poetical Prospect of Keswick* (1752). He wrote of a beautiful, fortunate, and prosperous land, where a miserly river poured its wealth into a broad lake and a land of rich harvests and noble woods:

> Here Derwent, like a miser, not content
> With narrow limits, spreads to vast extent;
> Where boats and islands make a pleasing sight,
> And yield at one both profit and delight.
> Here waves a harvest, there a noble wood,
> And yonder oxen graze all in the flood.[115]

Cowper's *Poetical Prospect* was not published until 1775, but it was composed just before Dalton's *Descriptive Poem*. It is thus interesting to read the two poems side by side, the one illuminating the other. Cowper's poem is the sort of celebration of the English countryside that might have been applied to any part of England by any one of the many poetasters who were proud of the peace and content of their local area. Its easy, undistinguished heroic couplets preach a moral message of contentment with God's world. Dalton's poem, by contrast, evokes an image of a landscape marked by the awful sublimity of the creator. Hence, his descriptions of Borrowdale as a place shaped by cataracts and storms and surveyed by ravenous birds of prey:

> The ravening kite, and bird of Jove,
> Which round the aerial ocean rove,

> And, floating on the billowy sky,
> With full expanded pennons fly,
> Their fluttering or their bleating prey
> Thence with death-dooming eye survey;
> Channels by rocky torrents torn,
> Rocks to the lake in thunder born,
> Or such as o'er our heads appear
> Suspended in their mid career,
> To start again at His command,
> Who rules fire, water, air, and land,
> I view with wonder and delight,
> A pleasing, tho' an awful sight[.][169]

The storm in the Vale of St John's to which Dalton refers was the subject of an article George Smith published in the *Gentleman's Magazine* in 1754. Smith described the deluge as 'a most dreadful storm of thunder and lightning, ... which bursting over the mountains, was attended with such a torrent of rain, as considerably changed the face of the country, and did incredible damage, in the vale below.'[170] The storm itself was so strong in the common memory that, twenty years later, William Gilpin, describing its effect on the Vale of St John's, portrayed it in very dramatic terms: 'This whole tract, we were told, was covered in an instant, with one continuous cascade of roaring torrent (an appearance which must have equalled the fall of Niagara) sweeping all before it from the top of the mountain to the bottom.'[171]

The interest in the destructive power of such natural phenomenon expressed by each of these writers is in part analytical, but it was also informed by classical leaning, painting, and landscape gardening, and by the developing aesthetic philosophy articulated by writers such as Edmund Burke. Burke explained his thoughts in *A Philosophical Enquiry into the Origin of Our Ideas of the Sublime and Beautiful* (1757). The beautiful, he explained,

Introduction

was associated with the desirable social passion of love and was seen in the small and the harmonious; it was, accordingly, felt to be feminine. The sublime, by contrast, was found in the self-preservative passion, in the sense of awe, and tended to the great, the uniform, the powerful, the obscure and the sombre, something that was, of its nature, very masculine.[172]

The landscape of Borrowdale came to epitomise these feelings in the minds of many visitors. A key text here, of course, was Brown's *Description of the Lake at Keswick*, which became a model for the aesthetic appreciation of the local terrain:

> Were I to analyse the two places into their constituent principles, I should tell you, that the full perfection of KESWICK consists of three circumstances, *Beauty, Horror,* and *Immensity* united; . . . But to give you a complete idea of these three perfections, as they are joined in KESWICK, would require the united powers of *Claude, Salvator,* and *Poussin*. The first should throw his delicate sunshine over the cultivated vales, the scattered cots, the groves, the lake, and wooded islands. The second should dash out the horror of the rugged cliffs, the steeps, the hanging woods, and foaming waterfalls; while the grand pencil of *Poussin* should crown the whole, with the majesty of the impending mountains.[173]

This is a description written by a man of a philosophical turn who loved the area deeply. He claimed that this 'accumulation of beauty and immensity tends not only to excite rapture but reverence; for my part I make an annual voyage to Keswick, not only as an innocent amusement, but a religious act'.[174] Brown may have known the area as a boy when he lived in Wigton, where his father was the vicar. He certainly knew it when he was a minor canon and later held a lectureship in Carlisle Cathedral. At that time, he was employed as a drawing master to William Gilpin, the son of Captain John Bernard Gilpin. John Bernard was a keen amateur artist and held sketching parties in the Lakes. He was also an enthusiastic amateur musician and convened parties at the Deanery where men, including Brown, Brownrigg, and Charles Avison (1710–1770), the Newcastle composer, played music and discussed aesthetic theory. Brown contributed a chapter on music and landscape to Avison's *Essay on Musical Expression* (1751), and it is possible to see how his ideas on music, art and landscape shaped his description of Borrowdale.

Brown's *Description* seems to have circulated as a letter within literary coteries, such as the circle of George Lyttelton, who were concerned with gardening and landscape aesthetics. It earned Brown the title of 'The Columbus of Keswick', but it was not until 1762 that a portion of the *Description* was published in a handful of metropolitan periodicals, including the *St James's Chronicle*, the *London Magazine*, and *Gentleman's and London Magazine*. Thereafter, it appeared as a chapbook in 1767, in Newcastle, and was reprinted in no fewer than four separate editions in Kendal, Whitehaven, and London between 1770 and 1772.[175] Portions of the text also circulated in collections such as Richard Cumberland's *Odes* (1770) and in Hutchinson's *History of Cumberland* (1794), where it appeared alongside Dalton's poem.

William Hutchinson had read John Dalton's poem in Pearch's anthology. He came to the Lakes apprised of the sensations appropriate to what he was about to see. Shaping his appreciation to his preconceptions, he described the landscape and his treasured impressions. He also gave an indication of how the tourist industry was developing in Keswick, both in the special experiences it could offer the eager tourist and the way it was ready to take advantage of his gullibility:

> Travellers who go in pursuit of pleasure to Keswick, are not unfortunate, if they fall upon the means of procuring the barge

Introduction

belonging [to] the Duke of Portland; a commodious vessel of four oars, which will hold a company of eight or ten persons, with lockers for the carriage of provisions and necessaries for a day's voyage; and also furnished with cannon for the echoes.[176]

Twenty years earlier John Dalton had also been sensitive to the quality of the visitor's experience of the landscape he was celebrating. In his 'Preface' he explicitly warned his readers that they might be disappointed by the recent clearing of the oak groves around Crow Park on the north-eastern shore of Derwentwater:

If, by the imperfect sketch in the following Poem, or by what he may elsewhere hear of the vale of Keswick and lake of Derwentwater, he should be induced to visit the Original, he must not confidently expect to see it exactly in the state described. For, if he goes thither . . . and expects to find the sylvan shrines of rural divinities wholly undisturbed and unprofaned, he will be much mistaken. Instead of that, he must prepare to be shocked at some late violations if those sacred woods and groves, which had, for ages shaded the side of the surrounding mountains, and (if prose be allowed the expression) the shores and promontories of that lovely lake.

These woodlands, which had grown up around the lake for more than a century, were one of the remnants of the estates of James Radcliffe (1689–1716), 3rd Earl of Derwentwater, who had been a leader in the Jacobite rising of 1715 and was executed for rebellion in 1716. The family's estates were confiscated and, in 1735, were granted to the Governors of the Royal Greenwich Hospital for Seamen. The Governors, as Derek Denman has observed, 'had a duty to maximise the economic return for the Hospital', and they found themselves obliged to sell 'the wood on the eastern shore and islands' of the lake.[177] The felling had

Fig. 12. Detail of Derwentwater: Sale of Timber *(c.1749)*

commenced in 1748, partly under the supervision of John Spedding's son, James (1719–1759), who was acting as agent of his father's timber business. An anonymous print of 1749 shows James directing the clearing in front of a vast expanse of Derwentwater fronted by long, narrow, and pointed mountains (Figure 12). When Thomas Smith of Derby painted the same view a few years later, the darkly dramatic prospect was unimpeded save for one blasted tree and one felled trunk (Figure 13).

Lowther, Fondly 'Familiar to the Sight'

John Dalton may also have felt a sense of loss when he revisited the valleys of the Lowther and the Eamont. These scenes, through which he transports the two young ladies in his poem, were ones he knew well as a schoolboy. The defining feature of this landscape is, of course, the River Lowther. The Lowther is a small stream

Fig. 13. Thomas Smith's Derwentwater from Crow Park *(1761)*

that drains the fells about Wet Sleddale and then flows north through the grounds of Shap Abbey and the village of Bampton before passing along the west side of the vast acreage of Lowther Park. It descends through limestone country, foaming with the lathering waters which may have given the stream its name, past the church and village of Askham, and, before it joins the River Eamont near the medieval bridge, it runs through the woods at Yanwath and Buckholme.[178] Dalton depicted this fertile landscape as a rural paradise:

> Here softly swells the spacious lawn,
> Where bounds the buck, and skips the fawn,
> Or, couch'd beneath the hawthorn-trees,
> In dappled groupes enjoy the breeze.[179]

The convention of revisiting rivers known in childhood was a fashionable literary topos in the eighteenth century.¹⁸⁰ So, it comes as little surprise that one discerns a sense of a personal recollection behind the decorous conventions of Dalton's verse. He, too, had reason to claim the Lowther as his native stream. His mother's family hailed from Lowther and his ancestors on his father's side had preached at Shap. As will be recalled, moreover, Dalton had studied under William Wilkinson (1685–1751) at Lowther College.

The school had been set up by Sir John Lowther of Lowther, 1st Viscount Lonsdale (1655–1700), in a redundant textile manufactory. Lowther, following the ideas of John Locke, considered that the pupils should not 'take up their time or incline their thoughts to poetry or fiction', but study history, chronology and the rudiments of mathematics as well as Latin, Greek and French in a regime where the discipline should be mild and gentle.¹⁸¹ Sir John himself had felt that the 'cruelty and blows' which he had received from his tutor, who was also his grandfather's butler, had done 'no good to [his] tender years'.¹⁸² The school he endowed was intended to be an innovatively modern educational institution, and was intended for 'none but gentlemen's sons', who were to devote themselves to 'the use and ornament of their country.'¹⁸³

As noted above, Sir John Clerk had made the long journey from Edinburgh to Lowther in 1731 to see his son George, who had been at the college for a year.¹⁸⁴ Sir John made a point of dining with Wilkinson, whom he described as 'a most polite, well bred man as ever I had seen'.¹⁸⁵ (They fared well on 'half a dussan of good dishes of meat, a botle of French wine and a botle of birtch wine', which was 'exceeding fine'.¹⁸⁶) After their meal, Wilkinson accompanied Clerk on a ride to Lowther Hall and around the Lowther estate. Even though the main house and the inner east wing had been gutted by a fire in the spring of 1718, Sir John was impressed:

Introduction

It has been a very large building of about 150 ft. in front but was accidentaly burnt down about sixteen years ago. The [steward], it seems, thought it was needless to sweep the chimnies but to let them take fire and clean themselves. By this practise a funnel which was near to some joysts, or which burst with the violence of the heat, set the whole house in fire which in less than two houres was burn'd to the ground. There perished in this fire a great dale of pictures and very fine furniture, particularely the paintings in the great hall by Vario which had cost above £1,000.[187]

The fire was reputed to have cost Lonsdale £30,000.[188] Sir Henry Lowther, who had inherited his father's title and estates from his own late brother, Richard (1692–1713), did not rebuild, and instead lived most of his time in London and at Bryam in Yorkshire. On his occasional visits to his Westmorland estate, he stayed in one of the remaining wings, as Sir John Clerk remarks:

I speak here only of the body of the house for the four wings were preserved. These stand two and two on each side of the house, two very near the house, and indeed so near that they never ought to have been there, and two at proper distances, in one of which my Lord lives and in another he keeps his horses which are very numerous of all kinds, particularly running horses.[189]

Celia Fiennes (1662–1741) had been overawed by the mansion when she rode up to Lowther on her side-saddle tour of England in 1698:

I went to it through fine woods, the front is just faceing the great roade from Kendall and Lookes very nobly, severall Rows of trees wch Leads to Large jron gates, open barres, into the stable yard wch is a fine building on ye one side of ye house very uniform, and just against it is such another Row of buildings ye other side of ye house Like two wings wch is the offices. Its built Each Like a fine house jutting out at Each End and ye middle is wth Pillars, white, and Carvings Like the Entrance of a building. These are just Equal and alike and Encompass the two sides of the first Court wch Enters, with Large jron gates and jron Palasadoes in the breadth, and then there is an ascent of 15 stone steps turned round, very Large, and on the top Large jron gates pallisad of jron betweene stone pillars, wch runs the breadth of the front. This Court is with paved walks of broad stone, one broad one to the house, ye other of same breadth runs a Crosse to the stables and offices, and so there is 4 Large Squares of grass in wch there is a large Statue of Stone in the midst of Each, and 4 Little Cupids or Little Boys in Each Corner of the 4 squares. Then one ascends severall more steps to another Little Court wth open Iron Railes, and this is divided Into severall grass plotts by paved walks of stone to the severall doores, some of wch are straight, others slope: the grass plotts being seven and in Each statue the middlemost is taller than the rest, this is just the front of ye house where you Enter a porch wth Pillars of Lime stone, but ye house is ye Red sort of stone of ye Country.[190]

As this description suggests, the house had been built to impress and, as it looked down the Lowther Valley towards the rivers Eamont and Eden and the Pennines beyond, it dominated the landscape, a worthy symbol of the Lowther's power and prestige. Sir Hugh Lowther (d.1338?) had emparked the manor after 1336. In 1630, the hall buildings had expanded from the ancient defensive three-storeyed peel tower on the east to include a hall, a great chamber and 'Severall Low ould roomes'.[191] Completing the motley array of buildings, there was another tower built in 1570 by Sir Richard Lowther (1532–1608).

Introduction

Such buildings did not match the status of Sir John Lowther (1582–1637), whose wealth, thanks to mortgages, demesne farming, legal practice, and trading ventures, was increasing rapidly in the peaceful years after the union of the two crowns. Nine years before his death in 1637, he set about constructing a central tower and a three-storeyed, five-bay facade between the two older towers. His son, Sir John Lowther, 1st Baronet of Lowther (1606 1676), added new wings and an outer court, new domestic offices and stables, a chapel and a gallery, and he beautified the hall porch with 'Pilosters and other cutt woork' carved in white stone.[192] When he succeeded in 1675 his grandson, Sir John (the 1st Viscount of Lonsdale), built new stable blocks, both 160 feet long and standing 272 feet apart. This Sir John was a minister in William III's cabinets, and he so benefitted from the profits of court and office that he wished to create a new mansion worthy of his estate and rank.

The old family house had stood 'in the Middle of the Village' and was, as Sir Ralph Thoresby was informed, replaced by 'such a palace-like fabric, as bears the bell away from all'.[193] Nevertheless it was to be 'Substantial and Warme, and yet hath as much Respect to Regular Architecture as is consistent with those two more Necessarie Qualities off a Northern hous.' [194] The house, the one later praised by Celia Fiennes, cost £7,000. It extended 220 feet from east to west; the inner and outer courtyards had a depth of some 330 feet. It was impressive. Had he still been alive, he would have no doubt taken a certain patrician pride when a bird's-eye prospect of Lowther, engraved by Johannes Kip (c.1653–c.1721), appeared in *Britannia Illustrata* (1707) (Figure 14).

This prospect shows the view of the Hall from the south with the terraced courtyards with their sculptures, which had so delighted Celia Fiennes. It stretches to the distant fells, the source of the Lowther, and shows the river flowing in its deeply cut valley to the

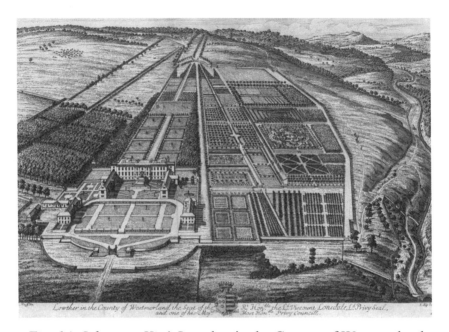

Fig. 14. Johannes Kip's Lowther in the County of Westmorland *(1707), after Leonard Knyff (1650–1722)*

west of the levelled park. The cultivated grounds recede beyond the hall in neatly packaged geometry, a pattern of well-ordered and regulated cultivation. The iron gates, the wide path, the ascent from terrace to terrace, and the final grand staircase to the state rooms on the *piano nobile* would have impressed many an aristocratic visitor.

The poet Thomas Tickell (1685–1740) knew Lowther and the Lowthers well, and like John Dalton half a century later, he had every reason to be lavish in his admiration. Thomas's grandfather, the aforementioned Thomas Tickell (c.1623–1692), had been estate steward to Sir James Lowther in Whitehaven, and the poet had spent his later childhood in the town and attended the school at St Bees conducted by his uncle William Jackson. In St Bees, Tickell was a friend of Sir John Lowther's eldest son, Richard, who had

Introduction

become 2nd Viscount Lonsdale after his father's death in 1700. Tickell dedicated his first published work *Oxford* (1706) to his friend, praising his ancestry, his stately seat, his manly character, and his feminine beauty:

> Whilst You, My Lord, adorn that stately Seat,
> Where shining Beauty makes her soft Retreat,
> Enjoying all those Graces, uncontroll'd,
> Which noblest Youths would die but to behold;
> Whilst You inhabit Lowther's awful Pile,
> A Structure worthy of the Founder's Toil,
> Amaz'd we see the former Lonsdale shine
> In each Descendant of his Noble Line,
> But most transported and surpriz'd we view
> His ancient glories all reviv'd in You,
> Where Charms, and Virtues join their equal Grace,
> Your Father's Godlike soul, your Mother's lovely Face.[195]

Later in the poem, Tickell describes the large decorative painting which adorned the spacious gallery on the north east front. The painting, the work of the Neapolitan artist Antonio Verrio (c.1639–1707) depicted *A Banquet of the Gods and the Four Seasons*. Verrio had been responsible for baroque decorative schemes in St George's Hall and elsewhere in Windsor Castle for Charles II and in the chapel at Whitehall for James II. James II employed him as 'principal Gardiner & Surveyor to the King', and he remodelled the gardens at Whitehall and St James's Palace after the pattern employed by André Le Nôtre (1613–1700) at Versailles.[196] For painting the hall, Seignior Verrio received £400 in addition to gold leaf, presents and his diet 'for near nine months'.[197] If Tickell's fulsome praise is anything to go by, it was money well-spent:

> Such Art as this adorns your Lowther's Hall,

> Where feasting Gods Carouse upon the Wall;
> The Nectar, which creating paint supplies,
> Intoxicates each pleas'd Spectator's Eyes;
> Who view, amaz'd, the Figures heavenly Fair,
> And think they breathe the true Elysian air.
> With Strokes so bold, great Varrio's hand has drawn
> The Gods in Dwellings, brighter than their own.[198]

There were other costs too. Fine prospects such as the one Lowther Hall came to command do not occur by chance: they need to be engineered. The high road was diverted and the 'mighty irregularities of the ground, and all that rock' were levelled, and, as Thomas Machell (c.1647–1698) described, the homes of the villagers needed to be moved. The old village of Lowther, explains Machell, 'was heretofore considerable, consisting of the hall, the church, the parsonage house, and seventeen tenements, messuages, and cottages, all of which were purchased by Sir John Lowther in the year 1682, and pulled down to enlarge his demesne, and open the prospect of his house, for they stood just in front of it.'[199] But not all vestiges of the ancient village were to be obliterated by the wide, tree-lined avenue which led from the rebuilt estate church to the grand terraces of the castle. Even today, beneath the turf, one can still trace the 'ghostly foundations of the cottages on either side of a village street'.[200]

The new village, Lowther Newtown, stands several hundred yards to the east of the ruined shell of the castle designed by Robert Smirke (1780–1867). Newtown consists of a series of small detached and semi-detached houses, built in grey-stone to a regular design set about a quadrangle of roads. It also contains the block that later became Lowther College. This country village can be seen in the *View of Lowther* which Matthias Read painted in the 1720s (Figure 15).[201] The hall, apparently undisfigured by the conflagration, still dominates the prospect, but on the left margin

Introduction

Fig. 15. Matthias Read's View of Lowther *(c.1725)*

of the picture is a rank of village cottages above the large, rectangular, neatly hedged fields. The vast well-ordered gardens have given way to woodland that clusters around the south side of the mansion. The River Lowther flows through a wooded valley beneath the mile-long terrace walk and across the front of the picture. It was to be almost a century before Lowther was rebuilt on an even grander scale by the ambitious Smirke, who would later design the British Museum.

A complementary account of the view depicted in Read's painting can be found in Sir John Clerk's account of his ride to Lowther in 1731:

On the east side of the house are large plantations of all kinds of timber, and on the west side are the gardens which have more of nature than art in them. The standard ewes and hedge ewes are very large and handsome, some being between 30 and 40 ft. high.

On the west side of the garden is a wilderness but what has lost much of its beuty by the height of the trees. Here are abundance of squirls which jump from tree to tree in a very merry way.[202]

The squirrels were jumping from tree to tree in an area where Kip's engraving shows a well-managed garden with its ornamental flower beds, its rows of vegetables, and its productive orchards. Sir John, a considerable land-owner himself, was impressed by the size of the estate. They were the finest grounds he had ever seen:

On the west side of this wilderness is a long walk which runs along the bank of a height and overlooks the windings of Louder Water and a very beutifull country diversified with hills and valies covered with wood.

At the back of the gardens on the south side are my Lord's parcks which are encompassed with a wall of dry stones about 10 ft. high and about seven or eight miles round. There are several divisions in this parck and above a thousand head of red and fellow deer. Here is likeways a fine breed of horses in several divisions and I think I counted above twenty mares and foals of this year and about sixty others. . . . As for black cattle they are keapt in inclosures and not in the parcks.

These parcks are the finest grounds I ever saw in my life. They lye for the most part high and are intermixed with very fine pieces of wood. The whole grounds lye upon a lyme stone which is seldom above a foot under the surface and crops out in long ranges in many places. The trees here are very luxuriant, for even the hazel bushes which are in great plenty are frequently 20 or 30ft. high.

We rode about these grounds for near three houres and

Introduction

amongst other things saw two large ponds on the higher grounds which, as I was told, were well stock'd with wild ducks, picke and pearch. Near to these ponds is a large summer house made for a musick or a dancing room, and here we have a fine prospect of a noble country seven miles round.[203]

The lord of this impressive manner, in Clerk's day, was Sir Henry Lowther, who (as noted above) inherited his late brother's estates in 1713. During the Jacobite rising of 1715, as Deputy Lieutenant of Westmorland, Sir Henry responded ably to the readying of the county's militia for the expected rebels. This militia, however, proved a less than effective force. On 2 November, as the Jacobites approached, the good men of Cumberland and Westmorland took to their heels. 'As soon as the news came,' Henry wrote afterwards, 'that the rebels were marching towards them, the posse ran off by hundreds.'[204] Undeterred, he rode off to help the defence of Penrith, and after the rebels proclaimed King James III in the town, Henry found himself 'hunted from place to place quite round the country'; a party of Jacobites even spent a night at Lowther Hall. He eventually found refuge in Appleby Castle.[205] In spite of the conduct of the men under his command, Sir Henry's loyalty to George I did not go unrewarded. For ten years after 1717, he held an influential position as one of the Gentlemen of the King's Bedchamber.

Having lost £30,0000 through the fire at Lowther, Henry lost nearly another £30,000 speculating on the South Sea Bubble in 1722, and he was forced to sell estates in Yorkshire and Durham.[206] He was a man prepared to gamble – and lose – heavily on both the stock market and the race track.

Working in conjunction with his much older cousin, Sir James Lowther in Whitehaven, he tightened the Lowther family's control on the politics of the two counties. Henry, himself, was appointed

Constable of the Tower of London and Lord Lieutenant of the Tower Hamlets and, having been made a Privy Councillor in 1726, he became Lord Privy Seal in Sir Robert Walpole's Cabinet in 1733. He had a deserved reputation for sound judgement and rectitude, but not for penetrating insight. Horace Walpole was his usual succinct self in summing up his character: 'He was a man of very conscientious and disinterested honour, a great disputant, a great refiner—no great genius.'[207] Sir Henry resigned three years later. According to Lord Egmont, he 'disliked the management of public affairs'; Henry, it was said, 'was out of humour with the world' and spent the next eighteen months in the South of France.[208] On his return to England, he lived with his widowed sister, Lady Ramsden, on her estate at Byram, in Yorkshire and left Lowther in the capable hands of his long-time agent, Richard Wordsworth (c.1690–1762), the poet's grandfather. In 1738, he was made Lord Lieutenant of Cumberland and Westmorland.

Sir Henry was, therefore, responsible for the county militia when the Jacobite rebels under Bonnie Prince Charlie marched south and, after a week-long siege, received the surrender of the city of Carlisle in November 1745. Lord Lonsdale, with a constitution so impaired by long illnesses that he could not 'bear either cold or fatigue' and unable to stay at Lowther because 'some alterations . . . were in hand', remained at his sister's house a hundred miles away in Yorkshire.[209] But he did efficient service as an intermediary, receiving daily reports and forwarding them to a grateful king. On 20 November an advance scouting party of Jacobites numbering 120 horse stayed the night at Lowther Hall and, three days later, Bonnie Prince Charlie himself made a brief pause there as he marched south to Derby. On 27 November, eighteen Jacobites from Carlisle, led by the son of the Earl of Kilmarnock, Charles Boyd (1728–1780), who had been a pupil at Lowther College, broke into Lowther Hall. As they were dining

Introduction

and carousing, however, they were assailed and roundly beaten by a party of thirty men from Penrith. Three of the rebels were killed and eleven taken prisoner.

Throughout his adult life, Sir Henry spent little time on his ancestral estate. In 1740, after Mr Wilkinson retired, Lowther College was closed. Lowther converted the building in Newtown, which had first been a carpet manufactory and then a school, into a factory for the washing of wool, which was then spun and combed in local cottages before being returned to the factory to be woven. Sir Henry thought that, as well as employing local people, it would 'not only do more good to the country but be more pleasing to the country in general as it will employ a good deal of the coarse wool and consume more provisions.'[210] The scheme was not a success, but the factory was reopened for the manufacture of linen goods which were exported to America through Whitehaven.

Sir Henry never married, and he died without issue in 1751. His cousin, Sir James Lowther of Whitehaven, also died unmarried in 1755, and his estates passed to his fourth cousin once removed, Sir William Lowther, 3rd Baronet of Marske. The following year, however, Sir William died – unmarried and without issue. Within five years the male line of three of the main branches of the Lowther family had become extinct. The patriarchal lineage which had, over the course of half a millennium, made the Lowther family a powerful oak presiding over Cumberland and Westmorland appeared to have lost its virility. The future of this family dedicated to acquiring estates, developing wealth, and maintaining its political power in the two counties seemed uncertain.

A legendary 400-year-old oak tree, known as 'Jak's Yak', in the grounds of Lowther Castle has come to symbolise the Lowther family. Its trunk is diseased, and its ageing branches are supported by wooden props for fear that they will break off under their own weight. John Dalton made his obeisance to that presiding oak even as one branch of the family had died, and another was nearing the end of its life:

> An oak for many an age has stood
> Himself a widely waving wood,
> While men and herds, with swift decay,
> Race after race, have passed away.[211]

The two young ladies who surveyed the vast estate from the caverns beneath the sea to the lawns of Lowther Castle were older sisters to the young man, Sir James Lowther, the future 1st Earl of Lonsdale, who would be required to sustain that central trunk.

This James Lowther was nine-years old when he inherited an estate worth £33,000 on the death of his father Robert Lowther of Maulds Meaburn in 1745.[212] In 1751, James inherited the estate, but not the title, of the late Viscount Lonsdale. The Baronet of Whitehaven's estates in Middlesex and Westmorland, worth £1,259, were left to James in 1755. In 1756, moreover, James received the rest of the late Baronet's vast fortune following the early death of Sir William Lowther of Holker Hall. As he attained his majority, James Lowther found himself 'perhaps the richest subject that His Majesty has.'[213] During Sir James's lifetime he sought to acquire further wealth and political power. He paid £55,000 for Charles Pelham's estate at Workington and the manors of Millom, Whicham, Greysouthen, and Clifton. These investments proved propitious; his profits from his collieries were £10,000 per annum in 1770 and were twice that when he died.[214]

He spent much of his money – well over £100,000 in total – seeking political influence. At his height nine parliamentary seats were under his direction. Popularly dubbed 'Sir James's Ninepins', these seats were Lowther's to play with as he saw fit, and through them he dominated the local politics of Cumberland and Westmorland. In 1784, a grateful William Pitt (1759–1806), to

Introduction

whom James had given the seat of Appleby, bestowed new titles on his patron, creating him Baron Lowther of Lowther, Baron of Kendal and Burgh, Viscount of Lonsdale and of Lowther, and Earl of Lonsdale.

In addition to his political investments, Sir James also applied his wealth in a handful of building projects. He extended Flatt Hall at Whitehaven, and he built a new planned village at Lowther. He also arranged for plans to be prepared for the development of Lowther Hall, and it is such a set of plans that Dalton praises in the poem that accompanies his *Descriptive Poem*: 'Some Thoughts on Building and Planting'. None of these plans, however, were ever put into effect.

During his lifetime, James acquired a reputation for being ferociously bad-tempered and over-bearing. He was seen as 'Jimmy, Grasp-all, earl of Toadstool' and as 'Wicked Jemmy'. A political opponent, the Revd. Alexander Carlyle, claimed he was 'more detested than any man alive as a shameless political sharper, a domestic bashaw, and an intolerant tyrant over his tenants and dependents.'[215] Lowther, Carlyle concluded, 'was truly a madman, though too rich to be confined.'[216]

In his final years, Sir James seems to have 'led a lonely' and confined 'existence at Lowther', where he died of 'a mortification of the bowels' on 24 May 1802.[217] He was 65. In 1761, he had married Lady Mary Stuart (1740–1824), the daughter of the 3rd Earl of Bute, but the marriage was without issue. The male line of the Lowthers of Maulds Meaburn was extinct. His estate passed to the Sir William Lowther, 2nd Baronet of Swillington (1757–1844).

Dalton's *Descriptive Poem*, which was published when Sir James was just 19, gives us but a glimpse of the life of this powerful and influential man. The poem, however, is dedicated to praising his family and the landscapes of the counties over which they presided. The ecstatic account of Skiddaw, with which Dalton concludes his description of Keswick, seems doubly meaningful in this regard:

> Supreme of mountains, Skiddow, hail!
> To whom all Britain sinks a vale!
> Lo, his imperial brow I see
> From foul usurping vapours free![218]

These lines pay tribute to one of the region's most iconic mountains, but they also analogically affirm the political order of the land and, moreover, the Lowthers' place at its summit. In applauding the majesty of Skiddaw, Dalton's verses project an image of the order of Georgian Britain – of its growing power, its expanding empire, its developing industry and commerce, and its vastly increasing wealth. This was an image of the Great Britain of King George II and a celebration of the country, of which, in the counties of Cumberland and Westmorland, the Lowther family continued to be the pinnacle.

Editorial Method

In preparing the texts included in this volume for publication, we have retained original spelling, capitalisation, and punctuation. Editorial insertions are placed in square brackets. We present Dalton's *Descriptive Poem* as a facsimile in order to retain the look of the original printed text. Readers should take note of certain conventions of eighteenth-century printing, including the use of the symbol ſ for the letter s: hence, almost appears as almoſt and state appears as ſtate. Contextual and explanatory notes including translations for Dalton's poem are listed by page and appear after the facsimile. Notes to the transcriptions of Weeks's and Cowper's poems in the appendices are included as endnotes.

Notes to the Introduction

1 William Hutchinson, *The History of the County of Cumberland*, 2 vols (Carlisle: F. Jollie, 1794), II, p. 233.
2 Peter Bicknell, *The Picturesque Scenery of the Lake District, 1752–1855: A Bibliography* (Winchester: St Paul's Bibliographies, 1990), p. 24.
3 The name of Dalton's mother is not listed in W.P. Courtney and John Wyatt's account of Dalton in the *Oxford Dictionary of National Biography*, 60 vols (Oxford: Oxford University Press, 2004), XIV, pp. 1013–14. The record of his parents' marriage is, however, documented in J. F. Haswell (ed.), *The Registers of Lowther, 1540–1812* (Penrith: 'Herald' Publishing Co. Ltd., 1933), p. 108: 'Mr. John Dalton Rectr. of Dean and Mrs. Elisabeth Clark of Lowther' (7 November 1706). For the date of Elizabeth's birth, see Haswell (ed.), *Registers of Lowther*, p. 45; for her death, see Samuel Jefferson, *The History and Antiquities of Cumberland: With Biographical Notices and Memoirs*, 2 vols (Carlisle: F. Jefferson, 1842), II, p. 388.
4 Joseph Foster (ed.), *Alumni Oxonienses: The Members of the University of Oxford, 1500–1714*, 3 vols (Oxford: Parker & Co., 1891), I, p. 368; R.W. Metcalfe, *The Ravenstonedale Parish Registers*, 3 vols (Kendal: T. Wilson, 1893–1894), III, p. vii; and B. Nightingale, *The Ejected of 1662 in Cumberland and Westmorland: Their Predecessors and Successors*, 2 vols (Manchester: Manchester University Press, 1911), II, p. 1110.
5 Nightingale, *The Ejected of 1662*, II, pp. 1191–96.
6 Foster (ed.), *Alumni Oxonienses, 1500–1714*, I, p. 368; Joseph Nicolson and Richard Burn, *The History and Antiquities of the Counties of Westmorland and Cumberland*, 2 vols (London 1777), I, p. 537.
7 Dalton had an elder sister, Jane, and three younger brothers: Jonathan, Henry, and Richard (see Jefferson, *History and Antiquities*, II, p. 388). Of these brothers, the only one whose career has been traced in detail is Richard (c.1715–1791), who went on to become one of the foremost illustrator of antiquities of the era, and was later appointed Keeper of the Pictures, Medals, and Books, and Antiquarian to his Majesty. Richard is also the 'Mr. Dalton' who is credited with having made 'the very exact Drawings' mentioned in first edition of Dalton's *Descriptive Poem*.
8 See W. A. J. Prevost, 'A Journie to Carlyle and Penrith in 1731', *Transactions of the Cumberland and Westmorland Antiquarian and Archaeological Society*,

n.s. 61 (1961), 202–37; and J. V. Beckett, 'Lowther College 1697–1740: "For none but gentlemen's sons"', *Transactions of the Cumberland and Westmorland Antiquarian and Archaeological Society*, n.s. 79 (1979), 103–7.

9 Prevost, 'Journie to Carlyle and Penrith', p. 215.

10 Joseph Foster (ed.), *Alumni Oxonienses: The Members of the University of Oxford, 1715–1886*, 4 vols (Oxford: Parker & Co., 1891), I, p. 334.

11 Senhouse, as noted above (p. 10), wrote in support of Dalton's bid to be elected Provost of Queen's College during the mid-1750s. See, notably, the letters Senhouse's correspondence with Katherine Lowther and Joseph Richmond between December 1753 and January 1754 (Carlisle Records Office, DSEN/5/5/1/4).

12 James Sambrook, 'Seymour (née Thynne), Frances, duchess of Somerset (1699–1754)', *Oxford Dictionary of National Biography*, 60 vols (Oxford: Oxford University Press, 2004), XLIX, pp. 880–81; James E. Tierney (ed.), *The Correspondence of Robert Dodsley, 1733–1764* (Cambridge: Cambridge University Press, 1988), p. 79.

13 Qt. in John Barnard (ed.), *Alexander Pope: The Critical Heritage* (London: Routledge & Keegan Paul, 1973), p. 247.

14 Horace Walpole to Lady Ossory, 3 August 1775: W. S. Lewis (ed.), *The Yale Edition of Horace Walpole's Correspondence*, 48 vols (New Haven, CT: Yale, 1937–1983), XXXII, pp. 243–44.

15 Walpole to Ossory, 10 December 1775: Lewis (ed.), *Walpole's Correspondence*, XXXII, pp. 283.

16 Lewis (ed.), *Walpole's Correspondence*, XXXII, pp. 243–44; see also, Stephen Bending, *Green Retreats: Women, Gardens and Eighteenth-Century Culture* (Cambridge: Cambridge University Press, 2013), pp. 207–9; see also *A Catalogue of the Collection of Eighteenth-Century Printed Books and Manuscripts formed by Lord Rothschild*, 2 vols (Cambridge: Privately printed at the University Press, 1954), I, p. 342.

17 Blaine Greteman, '"To Secure Our Freedom": How A Mask Presented at Ludlow-Castle Became Milton's Comus', in Blair Hoxby and Ann Baynes Coiro (eds), *Milton in the Long Restoration* (Oxford: Oxford University Press, 2016), pp. 143–58: pp. 143, 153.

18 See Greteman, '"To Secure Our Freedom"'.

19 *A New and General Biographical Dictionary: Containing an Historical, Critical, and Impartial Account of the Lives and Writings of the Most Eminent Persons in Every Nation in the World*, 12 vols (London: W. Strahan, 1795),

Introduction: Notes

IV, pp. 288–89: p. 288.

20 David Masson, *The Life of John Milton: Narrated in Connexion with the Political, Ecclesiastical, and Literary History of His Time*, 6 vols (London: Macmillan & Co., 1859–1880), VI, p. 760. The purchasing power conversion reported here was generated using the National Archives Currency Converter, 1270–2017, <http://www.nationalarchives.gov.uk/currency-converter/> (accessed 5 June 2018).

21 R. O. Bucholz, 'Semour, Charles, sixth duke of Somerset (1662–1748)', *Oxford Dictionary of National Biography*, 60 vols (Oxford: Oxford University Press, 2004), XLIX, pp. 857–60: p. 860.

22 John Dalton, *Two Epistles: The First, To a Young Nobleman from his Preceptor. Written in the year 1735–6. The second, To the Right Honourable the Countess of Hartford, At Percy Lodge: In the year 1744* (London: R. Dodsley, 1745), p. vi.

23 'Discourses on several Subjects and Occasions. By John Dalton, D.D.', *The Critical Review, or, Annals of Literature*, 6 (August 1758), 121–25: p. 125.

24 Frances Seymour (née Thynne), Countess of Hertford and Katherine Lowther (née Pennington) were both the great-granddaughters of Sir Henry Frederick Thynne (1615–1680). Their grandparents, Thomas Thynne (1640–1714) and Katherine Lowther (née Thynne), Viscountess Lonsdale (1653–1713) were siblings. See, Hugh Owen, *The Lowther Family: Eight Hundred Years of 'A Family of Ancient Gentry and Worship'* (Chichester: Phillimore & Co., 1990), pp. 64–5, 198–200.

25 Joseph Richmond to Humphrey Senhouse II, 22 December 1753: Papers of the Senhouse family of Netherhall, Maryport (Carlisle Records Office: DSEN/5/5/1/4).

26 Richmond to Senhouse (Carlisle Records Office: DSEN/5/5/1/4).

27 John Richard Magrath (ed.), *The Flemings in Oxford: Being Documents Selected from the Rydal Papers in Illustration of the Lives and Ways of Oxford Men, 1650–1700*, 3 vols (Oxford: Clarendon Press, 1904–1924), III, p. 441.

28 Margaret Lowther to James Lowther, 29 September 1755: Papers of the Lowther family (Carlisle Records Office: DLONS/L/1/1/60).

29 Owen, *The Lowther Family*, p. 48.

30 See, Sir James Lowther to Francis Gastrell, Lord Bishop of Chester, 30 October 1715 (Whitehaven RO, YDRC/10/38/8).

31 Sylvia Harcstark Myers, *The Bluestocking Circle: Women, Friendship, and the Life of the Mind in Eighteenth-Century England* (Oxford: Oxford

University Press, 1990), pp. 109–10.
32 'A List of Marriages for the Year 1750', *The Gentleman's Magazine*, 20 (February 1750), 91.
33 Catherine Talbot to Elizabeth Carter, 9 October 1762: Montagu Pennington (ed.), *A Series of Letters Between Mrs. Elizabeth Carter and Miss Catherine Talbot*, 4 vols (1809), III, pp. 22–24: p. 24.
34 Pennington, *Series of Letters*, p. 24.
35 'Bill of Mortality from June 28 to July 26, 1763', *The Gentleman's Magazine*, 33 (July 1763), 363; and 'Preferments', *The Royal Magazine* (August 1763), 112.
36 See, indicatively, 'Books publish'd in December; With Remarks', *The Gentleman's Magazine*, 24 (December 1754), 581; and 'A Descriptive Poem, addressed to Two Ladies, at their return from viewing the mines near Whitehaven', Monthly Review, 11 (December 1754), 487–89.
37 John Dalton, 'A Descriptive Poem, Addressed to Two Ladies at Their Return from Viewing the Mines near Whitehaven', in George Pearch (ed.), *A Collection of Poems in Two Volumes, by Several Hands*, 2 vols (London: G. Pearch, 1768), I, pp. 23–43.
38 For a concise discussion of the picturesque movement, see John Brewer, *The Pleasures of the Imagination: English Culture in the Eighteenth Century* (New York: Farrar, Straus & Giroux, 1997).
39 Bicknell, *Picturesque Scenery*, p. 22; see also, Cecilia Powell and Stephen Hebron (eds), *Savage Grandeur and Noblest Thoughts: Discovering the Lake District, 1750–1820* (Grasmere: Wordsworth Trust, 2010), pp. 42–43.
40 John Dalton, *A Descriptive Poem, Addressed to Two Ladies, at their Return from Viewing the Mines near Whitehaven* (London: J. and J. Rivington, 1755), p. 20; ll. 255–57. Horror, in this context, means something more akin to wonder than to the meaning conventionally ascribed to the word today.
41 Norman Nicholson, *The Lakers: The Adventures of the First Tourists* (London: Robert Hale, 1955), p. 28.
42 Myra Reynolds, *The Treatment of Nature in English Poetry Between Pope and Wordsworth* (Chiacgo: University of Chicago Press, 1896), p. 11.
43 Dalton, *Descriptive Poem*, p. 6; ll. 65–70.
44 The quotation marked in line 68 recalls *Paradise Lost*, II, 845–46. See also, on this point, Rudolph Beck, 'From Industrial Georgic to Industrial Sublime: English Poetry and the Early Stages of the Industrial Revolution', *British Journal for Eighteenth-Century Studies*, 27 (2004), 17–36.

Introduction: Notes

45 'A Descriptive Poem', *Monthly Review*, p. 489.
46 'Books publish'd', *Gentleman's Magazine*, p. 581.
47 Christopher Donaldson, Robert W. Dunning, and Angus J.L. Winchester (eds), *Henry Hobhouse's Tour Through Cumbria in 1774* (Kendal: Cumberland and Westmorland Antiquarian and Archaeological Society, 2018), p. 57. Tract Series, no. 27.
48 Thomas Amory, *The Life of John Buncle, Esq; Containing Various Observations and Reflections, Made in several Parts of the World, and Many Extraordinary Relations*, 2 vols (London: J. Johnson and B. Davenport, 1766), II, p. 213.
49 Nicolson and Burn, *Westmorland and Cumberland*, II, pp. 85–86; William Hutchinson, *The History of the County of Cumberland*, 2 vols (Carlisle: F. Jollie, 1794), II, pp. 54–56; and Thomas West, *A Guide to the Lakes*, 2nd edn (London: Richardson and Urquhart, 1780), pp. 197–98.
50 Bicknell, *Picturesque Scenery*, p. 33.
51 Daniel Defoe, *A Tour thro' the Whole Island of Great Britain, Divided into Circuits or Journies*, 3 vols. (London: G. Strahan, 1727), III, pp. 229–30.
52 Thomas Pennant, *A Tour in Scotland, and Voyage to the Hebrides, MDCCLXXII* (Chester: J. Monk, 1774), p. 53.
53 B. G. Hutton, 'A Lakeland Journey, 1759', *Transactions of the Cumberland and Westmorland Antiquarian and Archaeological Society*, n.s. 61 (1961), 288–93: p. 291.
54 Kenneth Morgan (ed.), *An American Quaker in the British Isles: The Travel Journals of Jabez Maud Fisher, 1775–1779* (Oxford: Oxford University Press, 1992), pp. 162–63.
55 Franklin to Jacques Barbeu-Dubourg, 12–16 November 1772: *Founders Online, National Archives* <https://founders.archives.gov/> (accessed 5 June 2018).
56 Country, in this context, is being used as a synonym for region or county.
57 Dalton, *Descriptive Poem*, pp. iii–iv.
58 Dalton, *Descriptive Poem*, pp. 14–15; ll. 159–80.
59 Samuel Johnson, 'Life of Denham', *Prefaces, Biographical and Critical, to the Works of the English Poets*, 10 vols (London: J. Nichols, 1779–1781), IV, pp. 1–31: p. 16.
60 David Fairer, 'Georgic', in Jack Lynch (ed.), *The Oxford Handbook of British Poetry, 1660–1800* (Oxford: Oxford University Press, 2016), pp. 457–72: p. 471.

61 Dalton, *Descriptive Poem*, p. 5; ll. 55–8.
62 Dalton, *Descriptive Poem*, p. vii.
63 Pearch (ed.), *Collection of Poems*, I, p. 23.
64 Dalton, *Descriptive Poem*, p. 16; ll. 181ff.
65 Dalton, *Descriptive Poem*, p. 23; ll. 306–11.
66 Dalton, *Descriptive Poem*, p. 24, ll. 316–17.
67 Dalton, *Descriptive Poem*, pp. 23–4; ll. 312, 318–25.
68 Order of Service for the Consecration of St. James Chapel, Whitehaven, 9am, 25 July 1753, p. 5 (Whitehaven Records Office, YPR17/121).
69 Order of Service for the Consecration of St. James Chapel, pp. 5–8.
70 Matthew Hyde and Nikolaus Pevsner, *Cumbria: Cumberland, Westmorland and Furness* (New Haven and London: Yale University Press, 2010), p. 673; see also, I. S. Nicholson and D. P. Sewell, 'History Notes on St. James's Church, Whitehaven', *Cumbria County History Trust* (2013), 37pp. <https://www.cumbriacountyhistory.org.uk/> (accessed 5 June 2018); and Frederick O'Dwyer, 'Robert West, Christopher Myers and St. James's Church, Whitehaven', *Journal of the Irish Georgian Society*, 12 (2010), 15–23.
71 Spedding to William Brown, 7 July 1752: qt. in J. V. Beckett, 'Carlisle Spedding (1695–1755), Engineer, Inventor and Architect', *Transactions of the Cumberland and Westmorland Antiquarian and Archaeological Society*, n.s. 83 (1983), 131–40: p. 135.
72 G. D. Burtchaell and T. U. Sadleir (eds), *Alumni Dublinenses*, new edn (Dublin: Alexander Thomas & Co., Ltd., 1935), p. 770; see also Beckett, 'Carlisle Spedding', p. 137.
73 Hyde and Pevsner, *Cumbria*, p. 674; and Nicholson and Sewell, 'History Notes', p. 16.
74 Pennant, *Tour in Scotland*, pp. 53–54.
75 See Nicholson and Sewell, 'History Notes', p. 8.
76 Hyde and Pevsner, *Cumbria*, p. 673. The purchasing power conversion reported here was generated using the *National Archives Currency Converter, 1270–2017*, <http://www.nationalarchives.gov.uk/currency-converter/> (accessed 5 June 2018).
77 Hyde and Pevsner, *Cumbria*, p. 673; and Nicholson and Sewell, 'History Notes', p. 28.
78 Angus Winchester and Mary Wane (eds), *Thomas Denton: A Perambulation of Cumberland 1678–1688* (Woodbridge: Boydell & Brewer, 2003), p. 105.

Introduction: Notes

79 Sylvia Collier and Sarah Pearson (eds), *Whitehaven 1660–1800: A New Town of the Late Seventeenth Century* (London: HMSO, 1991), p. 2; and J. V. Beckett, *Coal and Tobacco: The Lowthers and the Economic Development of West Cumberland, 1660–1760* (Cambridge: Cambridge University Press, 1981), pp. 181–89.
80 Collier and Pearson, *Whitehaven 1660–1800*, p. 2.
81 Nicolson and Burn, *Westmorland and Cumberland*, II, 42.
82 See Collier and Pearson, *Whitehaven 1660–1800*, p. 10.
83 Mary E. Burkett and David Sloss (eds), *Read's Point of View: Paintings of the Cumbrian Countryside* (Kendal: Skiddaw Press, 1995), pp. 60–68.
84 Beckett, *Coal and Tobacco*, p. 14; and Owen, *The Lowther Family*, pp. 237.
85 Beckett, *Coal and Tobacco*, p. 14. See also, Owen, *The Lowther Family*, pp. 237–38.
86 Beckett, *Coal and Tobacco*, p. 14. See also, Owen, *The Lowther Family*, pp. 237–38.
87 Owen, *The Lowther Family*, p. 238.
88 Collier and Pearson, *Whitehaven 1660–1800*, pp. 10, 26.
89 Beckett, *Coal and Tobacco*, p. 14.
90 Beckett, *Coal and Tobacco*, p. 20.
91 Beckett, *Coal and Tobacco*, p. 230.
92 John Lowther to William Christian, 27 December 1681: Carlisle Records Office (DLons/W2/1/16).
93 Owen, *The Lowther Family*, p. 242.
94 Beckett, *Coal and Tobacco*, p. 21.
95 Beckett, *Coal and Tobacco*, p. 21.
96 See David Cranstone, *Whitehaven Coast Archeological Survey*, Bound Report for the National Trust (2006–2007) <http://www.lakestay.co.uk/whitehavenmininghistory.html> (accessed 5 June 2018).
97 Thomas Tickell to Andrew Pellin, June/July 1688 (Carlisle Records Office D/LNS/W2/1/23/5): qt. in Collier and Pearson, *Whitehaven 1660–1800*, pp. 12–14, 30.
98 Beckett, *Coal and Tobacco*, p. 182.
99 Beckett, *Coal and Tobacco*, p. 183.
100 Beckett, *Coal and Tobacco*, p. 186.
101 Owen, *The Lowther Family*, p. 243.
102 Joseph Hunter (ed.), *The Diary of Ralph Thoresby, F.R.S.*, 2 vols (London:

From the Mines to the Mountains

H. Colburn and R. Bentley, 1830), I, p. 269.
103 Beckett, *Coal and Tobacco*, p. 20.
104 Owen, *The Lowther Family*, p. 252. The label 'richest commoner' was noted in John Clerk of Penicuik's account of his visit to Whitehaven in 1739; see, J. M. Gray (ed.), *Memoirs of the Life of John Clerk of Penicuik, Baronet* (Edinburgh: Scottish Historical Society, 1892), p. 153.
105 Nicolson and Burn, *Westmorland and Cumberland*, II, 43.
106 Beckett, *Coal and Tobacco*, pp. 230–31.
107 Beckett, *Coal and Tobacco*, p. 223.
108 Beckett, *Coal and Tobacco*, p. 57
109 Collier and Pearson, *Whitehaven 1660–1800*, p. 36.
110 W. A. J. Prevost, 'A Trip to Whitehaven to Visit the Coal-works There in 1739, By Sir John Clerk', *Transactions of the Cumberland & Westmorland Antiquarian & Archaeological Society*, n.s. 65 (1965), 305–19: p. 312.
111 Richard Warner, *A Tour through the Northern Counties of England*, 2 vols (Bath: R. Cruttwell, 1802), II, p. 121.
112 William King, *Political and Literary Anecdotes of His Own Times* (London: J. Murray, 1818), pp. 102–3.
113 John Wesley, *An Extract of the Reverend Mr. John Wesley's Journal, from July XX, 1750 to October 28, 1754* (London: J. Robinson and T. James, 1759), p. 88.
114 Wesley, *Journal*, pp. 88–89.
115 Beckett, *Coal and Tobacco*, p.18.
116 Sir James Lowther to Henry Newman, 9 May 1734: Society for the Promotion of Christian Knowledge (CR1/17/12655); qt. in Beckett, *Coal and Tobacco*, p.19.
117 J. V. Beckett, 'Illness and Amputation in the Eighteenth Century: The Case of Sir James Lowther', *Medical History*, 24 (1980), 88–92: 88–89.
118 Beckett, 'Carlisle Spedding', p.132.
119 J. D. Marshall, *Old Lakeland: Some Cumbrian Social History* (Newton Abbot: David & Charles, 1971), p. 66.
120 Beckett, *Coal and Tobacco*, p. 28.
121 Beckett, 'Carlisle Spedding', p.135.
122 Marshall, *Old Lakeland*, p.66
123 Beckett, 'Carlisle Spedding', p.132.
124 Beckett, 'Carlisle Spedding', p.132.

Introduction: Notes

125 J. S. Allen, 'The 1715 and other Newcomen Engines at Whitehaven, Cumberland', *Transactions of the Newcomen Society for the Study of the History of Engineering and Technology*, 44 (1975), 237–68: pp. 245–46.

126 William Stukeley, *Itinerarium Curiosum; Or, An Account of the Antiquities and Remarkable Curiosities in Nature or Art Observed in Travels Through Great Britain*, 2 vols. (London: Baker & Leigh, 1776), II, p. 52.

127 John Spedding to James Lowther, 8 March 1729: qt. in Jean E. Ward, 'The Sinking of Saltom Pit, Whitehaven', *Transactions of the Cumberland and Westmorland Antiquarian and Archaeological Society*, n.s. 91 (1991), 127–43: p. 127.

128 Beckett, 'Carlisle Spedding', p. 134.

129 Ward, 'The Sinking of Saltom Pit', p. 131.

130 Sir James Lowther, 'An Account of the Damp Air in a Coal-Pit, Sunk within 20 Yards of the Sea,' *Philosophical Transactions*, 429 (1753), 109–113: p. 109.

131 Lowther, 'An Account of the Damp Air', p. 110.

132 Lowther, 'An Account of the Damp Air', p. 111.

133 Lowther, 'An Account of the Damp Air', p. 111. This claim, of course, proved inaccurate and explosions caused by sparks did occur. See, John Sykes, *An Account of the Dreadful Explosion in Wallsend Colliery, on the 18th June, 1835* (Newcastle-upon-Tyne: J. Sykes, 1835), pp. 32–33.

134 Donaldson, et al., *Hobhouse's Tour Through Cumbria*, p. 42.

135 James Eyre Weeks, *A Poetical Prospect of the Coast Town and Harbour of Workington. To which is Annexed a Correct Edition of The Poetical Prospect Whitehaven* (Whitehaven: J. Weeks, 1752), pp. 15–16; ll. 61–8.

136 Ward, 'The Sinking of Saltom Pit', p. 134.

137 Ward, 'The Sinking of Saltom Pit', p. 137.

138 Ward, 'The Sinking of Saltom Pit', p. 137.

139 Ward, 'The Sinking of Saltom Pit', p. 137.

140 Joshua Dixon, *The Literary Life of William Brownrigg: To Which are Added An Account of the Mines Near Whitehaven* (London: Longman & Rees), p. 109.

141 Weeks, *A Poetical Prospect*, p. 17; ll. 92–101.

142 J. V. Beckett, 'An Eighteenth-Century Case History: Carlisle Spedding 1738', *Medical History*, 26 (1982), 303–6: p. 304.

143 Beckett, 'An Eighteenth-Century Case History', pp. 303–4.

144 Beckett, 'An Eighteenth-Century Case History', p. 305.
145 Weeks, *A Poetical Prospect*, pp. 8–9; ll. 154–61.
146 Herbert T. Pratt, 'Brownrigg, William (1711–1800)', *Oxford Dictionary of National Biography*, 60 vols (Oxford: Oxford University Press, 2004), VIII, pp. 274–75.
147 Beckett, 'Illness and Amputation'; see also, J. V. Beckett, 'Dr William Brownrigg, F.R.S.: Physician, Chemist and Country Gentleman', *Notes and Records of the Royal Society of London*, 31 (1977), 255–271: 257.
148 Beckett, 'Dr William Brownrigg'.
149 Beckett, 'Dr William Brownrigg', p. 258.
150 Christa Jungnickel and Russell K. McCormmach, *Cavendish* (Philadelphia, PA: The American Philosophical Society, 1996), pp. 155–56.
151 See Edward H. Davidson, 'Franklin and Brownrigg', *American Literature*, 23 (1951), 38–56.
152 Benjamin Franklin to Deborah Franklin, 14 July 1772: *Founders Online* (accessed 5 June 2018)
153 See, indicatively, Donaldson, et al, *Hobhouse's Tour Through Cumbria*, pp. 14–19.
154 Benjamin Franklin to Jacques Barbeu-Dubourg, 12–16 November 1772: *Founders Online* (accessed 5 June 2018)
155 Benjamin Franklin to Jean-Louis Giraud Soulavie, 22 September 1782: *Founders Online* (accessed 5 June 2018)
156 Pennant, *A Tour of Scotland*, pp. 53–55.
157 The quotation is from Milton's *Comus* (l. 435). See John Milton, *Complete Shorter Poems*, ed. by Stella P. Revard (Oxford: Wiley-Blackwell, 2009), p. 202.
158 Pennant includes a footnote here: 'The Germans believed in two species [of mine fairy]; one fierce and malevolent, the other a gentle race, appearing like little old men, dressed like the miners, and not much above two feet high: these wander about the drifts and chambers of the works, seem perpetually employed, yet do nothing; some seem to cut the ore, or fling what is cut into vessels, or turn the windlass; but never do any harm to the miners, expect provoked: as the sensible Agricola, in this point credulous, relates in his book, de Animatibus subterraneis' (Pennant, *Tour of Scotland*, p. 56).
159 Pennant includes a footnote here, referencing John Grubb's comic ballad 'St. George for England', which was included in Thomas Percy's *Reliques of Ancient English Poetry*, 2nd edn, 3 vols (London: J. Dodsley, 1767), III, pp.

311–27. The relevant lines, describing Pendragon, run: 'Itch, and Welsh blood did make him hot, | And very prone to ire; H' was ting'd with brimstone, like a match, | And would as soon take fire: | As brimstone he took inwardly | When scurf gave him occasion, | His postern puff of wind was a | Sulphureous exhalation' (ll. 35–42).

160 Pennant, *A Tour of Scotland*, pp. 55–57.

161 Pennant, *A Tour of Scotland*, p. 48.

162 Ian Tyler, *Goldscope and the Mines of Derwent Fells* (Keswick: Blue Rock Publications, 2005), pp. 57–149.

163 William Rollinson, *A History of Man in the Lake District* (London: J. M. Dent & Sons, 1967), p. 125.

164 George Smith, 'Journey to the Black Lead Mines', *Gentleman's Magazine*, 21 (1751), 51–53: 53.

165 Smith, 'Journey to the Black Lead Mines', p. 53.

166 Pennant, *A Tour of Scotland*, pp. 55–57.

167 Denton, *Perambulation of Cumberland*, p. 135.

168 Thomas Cowper, *A Poetical Prospect of Keswick, and the Parts Adjacent, Written in the Spring of the Year 1752* (Cockermouth: T. Bailey and Son, 1851), p. 5; ll. 72–77.

169 Dalton, *Descriptive Poem*, pp. 20–21; ll. 264–77.

170 George Smith, 'A Dreadful Storm in Cumberland', *Gentleman's Magazine*, 24 (1754), 464–65: p.464.

171 William Gilpin, *Observations, Relative Chiefly to Picturesque Beauty, Made in the Year 1772*, 2 vols (London: R. Blamire, 1786), II, p. 37.

172 Edmund Burke, *Philosophical Enquiry into the Origins of Our Idea of the Beautiful and the Sublime* (London: R. and J. Dodsley, 1757), pp. 41–115.

173 John Brown, *A Description of the Lake at Keswick* (Newcastle, 1767).

174 Qt. in Richard Cumberland, *Odes* (London: J. Robson, 1776), p. 6.

175 See Bicknell, *Picturesque Scenery*, p. 24.

176 William Hutchinson, *An Excursion to the Lakes in Westmorland and Cumberland; With a Tour through Part of the Northern Counties in the Years 1773 and 1774*, 2 vols (London: J. Wilkie, 1776), II, pp. 175–75.

177 Derek Denman, *Materialising Cultural Value in the English Lake District: A Study of the Responses of New Landowners to Representations of Place and People*, Unpublished PhD thesis (Lancaster University, 2011), p. 19; see also, pp. 77–97.

178 Diane Whaley, *A Dictionary of Lake District Place Names* (Nottingham: English Place Names Society, 2006), p. 226.
179 Dalton, *Descriptive Poem*, pp. 16–17; ll. 199–202.
180 See David Fairer, *Organising Poetry: The Coleridge Circle, 1790–1798* (Oxford: Oxford University Press, 2009), pp. 95–117.
181 Beckett, 'Lowther College', p. 104.
182 J. V. Beckett, 'Lowther, John, first Viscount Lonsdale (1655–1700)', *Oxford Dictionary of National Biography*, 60 vols (Oxford: Oxford University Press, 2004), XXXIV, pp. 634–36.
183 Beckett, 'Lowther College 1697–1740', p. 104.
184 Prevost, 'A Journie to Carlyle and Penrith', p. 206.
185 Prevost, 'A Journie to Carlyle and Penrith', p. 209.
186 Prevost, 'A Journie to Carlyle and Penrith', p. 210.
187 Prevost, 'A Journie to Carlyle and Penrith', p. 211.
188 Owen, *The Lowther Family*, p. 225.
189 Prevost, 'A Journie to Carlyle and Penrith', p. 211.
190 Celia Fiennes, *Through England on a Side Saddle in the Time of William and Mary* (London: Field and Tuer, 1888), pp. 166–67.
191 M. H. Port, 'Lowther Hall and Castle', *Transactions of the Cumberland and Westmorland Antiquarian and Archaeological Association*, n.s. 81 (1981), 123–36: p. 123.
192 Port, 'Lowther Hall and Castle', p. 123.
193 Port, 'Lowther Hall and Castle', p. 125.
194 Port, 'Lowther Hall and Castle', p. 125.
195 Thomas Tickell, *Oxford: A Poem* (London: E. Sanger, 1707), p. 1; ll. 1–12.
196 Lindsay Stainton and Christopher White, *Drawing in England from Hilliard to Hogarth* (London: British Museum Publications, 1988), pp. 172–73.
197 Port, 'Lowther Hall and Castle', p. 126.
198 Tickell, *Oxford*, p. 3; ll. 123–30.
199 P. J. Mannex, *History, Topography and Directory of Westmorland* (London: Simpkin, Marshall & Co., 1849), p. 229
200 Roy Millward and Adrian Robinson, *The Lake District* (London: Eyre and Spottiswoode, 1970), p. 198.
201 Burkett and Sloss, *Read's Point of View*, p. 47.
202 Prevost, 'A Journie to Carlyle and Penrith', pp. 212–14.
203 Prevost, 'A Journie to Carlyle and Penrith', p. 212.

Introduction: Notes

204 Owen, *The Lowther Family*, p. 224.
205 Owen, *The Lowther Family*, p. 224.
206 Owen, *The Lowther Family*, p. 225; and J. V. Beckett, 'Lowther, Henry, 3rd Viscount Lonsdale (1694–1751)', *Oxford Dictionary of National Biography*, 60 vols (Oxford: Oxford University Press, 2004), XXXIV, p. 636.
207 Horace Walpole, *Memoires of the Last Ten Years of the Reign of George the Second*, 2 vols (London: J. Murray, 1822), I, p. 17.
208 Owen, *The Lowther Family*, p. 226.
209 Owen, *The Lowther Family*, p. 229.
210 Owen, *The Lowther Family*, p. 230.
211 Dalton, *Descriptive Poem*, pp. 20–21; ll. 264–77
212 J. V. Beckett, 'Inheritance and Fortune in the Eighteenth Century: The Rise of Sir James Lowther, Earl of Lonsdale', *Transactions of the Cumberland and Westmorland Antiquarian and Archaeological Association*, n.s. 87 (1987), 171–78: p. 175.
213 Owen, *The Lowther Family*, p. 283.
214 J. V. Beckett, 'Lowther, James, earl of Lonsdale (1736–1802)', *Oxford Dictionary of National Biography*, 60 vols (Oxford: Oxford University Press, 2004), XXXIV, pp. 625–28: p. 627.
215 Beckett, 'Lowther, James, earl of Lonsdale (1736–1802)', p. 628.
216 Beckett, 'Lowther, James, earl of Lonsdale (1736–1802)', p. 628.
217 Owen, *The Lowther Family*, p.302; and Beckett, 'Lowther, James, earl of Lonsdale (1736–1802)', p. 628.
218 Dalton, *Descriptive Poem*, p. 22; ll. 298–91.

From the Mines to the Mountains

A Facsimile of Dalton's
Descriptive Poem
(1755)

From the Mines to the Mountains

A DESCRIPTIVE POEM,

ADDRESSED TO

TWO LADIES,

At their RETURN from Viewing

The MINES near WHITEHAVEN.

To which are added,

SOME THOUGHTS ON BUILDING and PLANTING,

TO

Sir James Lowther, of Lowther-Hall, Bart.

By JOHN DALTON, D.D.

LONDON:
Printed for J. and J. RIVINGTON in St. Paul's Church-yard, and R. and J. DODSLEY in Pall-Mall.
MDCCLV.

PREFACE.

THE following Poem was written almost two years ago, and was not intended for the press: but the approbation, with which several friends of the author have perused it, now encourages him to offer it to the public. It was owing to the strong inclination, by which he was prompted to express the pleasure he had received, in a visit paid to his native country after a long absence, from the view of the several uncommon, grand, or beautiful scenes of nature and of art, which he here attempts to describe. This pleasure was undoubtedly much heightened by an advantagious comparison of its present state with That, in which he had left it. When we behold rich improvements of a wild and uncultivated soil, in their state of maturity, without having observed their rise and progress, we are struck with wonder and astonishment, to' see the face of Nature totally changed. It carries an air of enchantment and romance: and the fabulous and luxuriant description, given us by the Poet, of yellow harvests rising up instantaneously under the wheels of the chariot of Ceres, as it passed over the barren deserts, hardly seems, in the midst of our surprise, too extravagant an image to represent the greatness and seeming suddenness of such a change:

————————cano rota pulvere labens
Sulcatam fæcundat humum; flavescit aristis
Orbita; surgentes condunt vestigia culmi.
Vestit iter comitata seges.—— *Claudian.*

But how great and rational soever the pleasure of such a sight may be, it is still surpassed by that arising from the extraordinary increase of a trading Town, and new plantations of Houses and Men. Such was the satisfaction the author felt at the appearance of the town and harbour of Whitehaven, after an absence of somewhat less than thirty years. The Mines near that place are remarkable for so many singular circumstances, that they are generally esteemed to be well worth the observation of travellers. But the uncommonness of the occasion, on which this description was addressed to two very amiable Persons, afforded him the means of still heightening the novelty of his subject, and of throwing it into a more agreeable and poetic light by an easy introduction of classical allusion and parody *. It also gave him (what he va-

---

Allusion and parody, &c.] To save the reader the trouble of turning to books, several of the passages alluded to in the description of the mines are here inserted:

———————— quæ te fortuna fatigat,
Ut tristes sine sole domos, loca turbida, adires?
Virg. Æn. VI.

lued

lued most) a natural opportunity of expressing his just esteem for a truly respectable family, with whose merit he had long had the happiness of being well acquainted, whose Interest appears to be inseparably connected with That of his native country, and to which It already owes the most considerable advantages.

The admirers of the extensive knowledge, unspotted honour, public spirit, and firm adherence to the great and essential interests of the British constitution and Protestant Succession, by which the late Lord

> At cantu commotæ Erebi de sedibus imis
> Umbræ ibant tenues, simulacraq; luce carentum—
> Quin ipsæ stupuere domus, atq; intima Lethi
> Tartara, cœruleosq; implexæ crinibus angues
> Eumenides; tenuitq; inhians tria Cerberus ora;
> Atq; Ixionii cantu rota constitit orbis.
> Virg. Georg. Lib. IV. Ver. 471.

> Nulla sit immunis regio, nullumq; sub umbris
> Pectus inaccessum Veneri. Jam tristis Erynnis
> Sentiat ardores: Acheron, Ditisq; severi
> Ferrea lascivis mollescant corda sagittis.
> Claud. de Rap. Pros. Lib. I. Ver. 121.

> —————————— divino semita gressu
> Claruit.——
> Ibid.

> Hinc exaudiri gemitus, & sæva sonare
> Verbera: tum stridor ferri, tractæq; catenæ.
> Virg. Æn. Lib. VI. Ver. 557. & passim

> Hinc via Tartarii quæ fert Acherontis ad undas—
> Turbidus hinc cœno rastaq; voragine gurges
> Æstuat, atq; omnem Cocyto eructat arenam.
> Virg. Æn. Lib. VI.

Lonsdale

Lonsdale was universally distinguished, may perhaps be offended at the author's confining himself, in what he here says of his Lordship, to his provincial character, to his improvements in husbandry, and his endeavours to introduce manufactures into his own country. His excuse must be, that this was the part of his Lordship's Character which came most properly within the compass of his subject. Besides, if the light in which he has endeavoured to place his Example in that particular, could, in any degree, contribute to engage the imitation of young persons of the same rank and fortune in other places, he might then hope that the moral of his poem would appear to be not merely provincial, but national.

For, during the present melancholy condition, even in an age eminent for charity, of the numerous unemployed Poor of this kingdom, and the experienced and acknowledged inability of the present laws to provide for their effectual employment at home, and prevent their crouding to this their great school of idleness and vice, the Metropolis, what can we hope for, to alleviate this misery, but that Noblemen and Gentlemen of considerable estates, daily growing more sensible of the necessity of such a conduct, will lend a like generous attention to the ignorance and poverty of their respective countrymen?—This, as far as the author can presume to judge of so difficult a matter, appears to be the best that can be done, untill the Legislature shall be so happy as to accomplish that great end by some such simple yet comprehensive plan, as was, in a late session of parliament, recommended to their consideration by a Noble Earl;

and

and which met with their most favourable reception at that time, though it has not yet received the sanction of a law.

This Preface must not conclude without a precaution to the Reader, which may possibly prevent his meeting with an unpleasing disappointment. If, by the imperfect sketch in the following Poem, or by what he may elsewhere hear of the vale of Keswick and lake of Derwentwater, he should be induced to visit the Original, he must not confidently expect to see it exactly in the state described. For, if he goes thither with an imagination glowing warm with classical enthusiasm, and expects to find the sylvan shrines of the rural divinities wholly undisturbed and unprofaned, he will be much mistaken. Instead of that, he must prepare to be shocked at some late violations of those sacred woods and groves, which had, for ages, shaded the sides of the surrounding mountains, and (if prose may be allowed the expression) the shores and promontories of that lovely lake. For,

> Where the rude axe with heaved stroke
> Was never heard the Nymphs to daunt,
> Or fright them from their hallow'd haunt,

there, alas, is now,

> The lonely mountains o'er,
> And the resounding shore,

A

[viii]

  A voice of weeping heard and loud lament;
   From haunted spring and dale,
   Edg'd with poplar pale,
  The parting Genius is with sighing sent:
  With flower-inwoven tresses torn,
  The Nymphs in twilight shade of tangled thickets mourn.

However, for his consolation, he may still, notwithstanding all those profanations, hope to find there an assemblage of such exquisite though different beauties, as will well deserve to be admired by him; as well perhaps as any one part of the inanimate creation.

TO

TO
TWO LADIES

At their RETURN from Viewing

The MINES near WHITEHAVEN.

WELCOME to light, advent'rous pair!
Thrice welcome to the balmy air
From sulphurous damps in caverns deep,
Where subterraneous thunders sleep,
Or, wak'd, with dire Ætnæan sound   5
Bellow the trembling mountain round,

From sulphurous damps, &c.] The coal mines near Whitehaven are greatly infested with fulminating damps; large quantities of them being frequently collected in those deserted works, which are not ventilated with perpetual currents of fresh air: and, in such works, they often remain for a long time, without doing any

Till to the frighted realms of day,
Thro' flaming mouths they force their way;
From bursting streams, and burning rocks,
From nature's fierce intestine shocks; 10
From the dark mansions of despair
Welcome once more to light and air!

 B u t why explore that world of night
Conceal'd till then from female sight?
Such grace and beauty why confine 15
One moment to a dreary mine?

 W a s it because your curious eye
The secrets of the Earth would spy,

---

mischief. But when, by some accident, they are set on fire, they then produce dreadful explosions, very destructive to the miners; and bursting out of the pits with great impetuosity, like the fiery eruptions from burning mountains, force along with them ponderous bodies to a great height in the air.

From burning rocks, &c.] The coal in these mines hath, several times, been set on fire by the fulminating damp, and hath continued burning for many months; until large streams of water were conducted into the mines, and suffered to fill those parts where the coal was on fire. By such fires, several collieries have been intirely destroyed; of which there are instances near Newcastle, and in other parts of England, and in the shire of Fife in Scotland; in some of which places, the fire has continued burning for ages. But more mines have been ruined by inundations.

How

How intervein'd rich minerals glow,
How bubbling fountains learn to flow? 20
  Or rather that the sons of day
Already own'd your rightful sway,
And therefore, like young Ammon, you
Another world would fain subdue?
  What tho' sage Prospero attend, 25
While you the cavern'd hill descend,
Tho', warn'd by him, with bended head
You shun the shelving roof, and tread
With cautious foot the rugged way,
While tapers strive to mimic day? 30
Tho' he with hundred gates and chains
The Demons of the mine restrains,

The demons of the mine restrains, &c.] In order to prevent, as much as possible, the collieries from being filled with those pernicious damps, it has been found necessary carefully to search for those crevises in the coal, from whence they issue out; and at those places, to confine them within a narrow space; and from those narrow spaces in which they are confined, to conduct them through long pipes into the open air; where being set on fire, they consume in perpetual flames, as they continually arise out of the earth.

To whom their parent, jealous Earth,
To guard her hidden stores gave birth,
At which, while kindred furies sung, 35
With hideous joy pale Orcus rung;
Tho' boiling with vain rage they sit
Fix'd to the bottom of the pit,
While at his beck the spi'rits of air
With breath of heaven their taints repair; 40
Or if they seek superior skies,
Thro' ways assign'd by him they rise,
Troop after troop at day expire
In torments of perpetual fire;
Tho' he with fury-quelling charms 45
The whole infernal host disarms,
And summons to your guarded sides
A squadron of etherial guides,

And summons, &c.] Those who have the direction of these deep and extensive works, are obliged to use great care and art in keeping them continually ventilated with perpetual currents of fresh air; which afford the miners a constant supply of

You

You still, when we together view
The dreadful enterprize and you, 50
The public care and wonder go
Of all above and all below.

FOR at your presence toil is o'er,
The restless miner works no more.
Nor strikes the flint, nor whirls the steel 55
Of that strange spark-emitting wheel,
Which, form'd by Prospero's magic care,
Plays harmless in the sulphurous air;

that vital fluid, and expel out of the mines damps and other noxious exhalations, together with such other burnt and foul air, as is become poisonous and unfit for respiration.

Nor strikes the flint, &c.] It having been observed, by Mr. Spedding, who superintends these collieries, and to whom the author here gives the name of Prospero, that the fulminating damp could only be kindled by flame, and that it was not liable to be set on fire by red-hot iron, nor by the sparks produced by the collision of flint and steel, he invented a machine, in which while a steel wheel is turned round with a very rapid motion, and flints are applied thereto, great plenty of fiery sparks are emitted, that afford the miners such a light as enables them to carry on their work in close places, where the flame of a candle, or lamp, would occasion dreadful explosions. Without some invention of this sort, the working of these mines, so greatly annoyed with these inflameable damps, would long ago have been impracticable.

Without

Without a flame diffuses light,
And makes the grisly cavern bright.   60
His task secure the miner plies,
Nor hears Tartarian tempests rise;
But quits it now, and hastes away
To this great Stygian holiday.

 Agape the sooty collier stands,   65
His axe suspended in his hands,
His Æthiopian teeth the while
" Grin horrible a ghastly smile,"
To see two goddesses so fair
Descend to him from fields of air.   70
Not greater wonder seiz'd th' abode
Of gloomy Dis, infernal god,
With pity when th' Orphēan lyre
Did ev'ry iron heart inspire,
Sooth'd tortur'd ghosts with heavenly strains,   75
And respited eternal pains.

          But

But on you move thro' ways less steep
To loftier chambers of the deep,
Whose jetty pillars seem to groan
Beneath a ponderous roof of stone.   80
Then with increasing wonder gaze
The dark inextricable maze,
Where cavern crossing cavern meets,
(City of subterraneous streets!)
Where in a triple story end   85
Mines that o'er mines by flights ascend.

But on you move, &c.] The reader may suppose that he hath entered these mines by an opening at the bottom of a hill, and hath already passed through a long adit, hewn in the rock, and arched over with brick, which is the principal road into them for men, and for horses; and which, by a steep descent, leads down to the lowest vein of coal. Being arrived at the coal, he may suppose himself still to descend, by ways less steep, till, after a journey of a mile and a half, he arrives at the profoundest parts of the mine. The greatest part of this descent is through spacious galleries, which continually intersect other galleries; all the coal being cut away except large pillars, which, in deep parts of the mine, are three yards high, and about twelve yards square at the base; such great strength being there required to support the ponderous roof.

A triple story, &c.] There are here three strata of coal, which lie at a considerable distance one above another. The mines wrought in these parallel strata have a communication by pits, and are compared by the author to the different stories of a building.

But

But who in order can relate
What terrors ſtill your ſteps await?
How iſſuing from the ſulphurous coal
Thick Acherontic rivers roll? 90
How in cloſe center of theſe mines,
Where orient morning never ſhines,
Nor the wing'd Zephyrs e're reſort,
Infernal Darkneſs holds her court?
How, breathleſs, with faint pace, and ſlow, 95
Thro' her grim ſultry realm you go,
Till purer riſing gales diſpenſe
Their cordials to the ſick'ning ſenſe?

Thick Acherontic rivers, &c.] The water that flows from the coal is collected into one ſtream, which runs towards the fire-engines. This water is yellow and turbid, from a mixture of ocher, and ſo very corroſive, that it quickly conſumes iron.

How, breathleſs, with faint pace, and ſlow, &c.] Thoſe who deſcend into theſe mines, find them moſt cloſe and ſultry in the middle parts, that are moſt remote from the pits and adits, and perceive them to grow cooler the nearer they approach to thoſe pits which are ſunk to the deepeſt parts of the mines; down which pits, large ſtreams of freſh air are made to deſcend, and up which, the water is drawn out, by means of fire-engines.

Your

Your progress next the wondering muse
Thro' narrow galleries pursues;   100
Where Earth, the miner's way to close,
Did once the massy rock oppose:
In vain: his daring axe he heaves,
Tow'ards the black vein a passage cleaves:
Dissever'd by the nitrous blast,   105
The stubborn barrier bursts at last.
Thus, urg'd by Hunger's clamorous call,
Incessant Labour conquers all.

Where Earth, &c.] The vein of coal is not always regularly continued in the same inclined plain, but, instead thereof, the miners frequently meet with hard rock, which interrupts their further progress. At such places there seem to have been breaks in the earth, from the surface downwards; one part of the earth seeming to have sunk down, while the part adjoining has remained in its antient situation. In some of these places, the earth may have sunk ten or twenty fathoms, or more; in other places, less than one fathom. These breaks, the miners call *Dykes*; and when they come at one of them, their first care is to discover whether the strata in the part adjoining be higher or lower than in the part where they have been working; or (to use their own terms) whether the coal be cast down, or cast up. If it be cast down, they sink a pit to it; but if it be cast up to any considerable height, they are oftentimes obliged, with great labour and expence, as at the place here described, to carry forwards a level or long gallery thro' the rock, until they again arrive at the stratum of coal.

IN spacious rooms once more you tread,
Whose roofs with figures quaint o'erspread 110
Wild nature paints with various dyes,
With such as tinge the evening skies.

A different scene to this succeeds:
The dreary road abruptly leads
Down to the cold and humid caves, 115
Where hissing fall the turbid waves.
Resounding deep thro' glimmering shades
The clank of chains your ears invades.
Thro' pits profound from distant day
Scarce travels down light's languid ray. 120
High on huge axis heav'd, above,
See ballanc'd beams unweary'd move!

Whose Roofs, &c.] These colours, with which the free-stone roof of the mines is beautifully variegated in many places, and which have the appearance of clouds, seem to proceed from exsudations of salts, ocher, and other earthy substances.

While

While pent within the iron womb
Of boiling caldrons pants for room
Expanded Steam, and shrinks, or swells,   125
As cold restrains, or heat impells,

While pent within the iron womb, &c.] The author hath here taken occasion to celebrate the fire-engine, the invention of which does such honour to this nation. He has endeavoured to describe, in a poetic manner, the effects of the elastic steam, and the great power of the atmosphere; which, by their alternate actions, give force and motion to the beam of this engine, and by it, to the pump-rods, which elevate the water through tubes, and discharge it out of the mine. It appears, from pretty exact calculations, that it would require about 550 men, or a power equal to that of 110 horses, to work the pumps of one of the largest fire-engines now in use, (the diameter of whose cylinder is seventy inches) and thrice that number of men to keep an engine of this size constantly at work. And that as much water may be raised by an engine of this size kept constantly at work, as can be drawn up by 2520 men with rollers and buckets, after the manner now daily practised in many mines; or as much as can be borne up on the shoulders of twice that number of men; as is said to be done in some of the mines of Peru.—So great is the power of the air in one of those engines.

There are four fire-engines belonging to this colliery; which, when all at work, discharge from it about 1228 gallons every minute, at thirteen strokes; 1,768,320 gallons every twenty-four hours. By the four engines here employed, nearly twice the above-mentioned quantity of water might be discharged from mines that are not above sixty or seventy fathoms deep, which depth is rarely exceeded in the New-castle collieries, or in any of the English collieries, those of Whitehaven excepted.

The reader may find an account of Savery's engine in Harris's Lexicon Technicum.—Many great improvements have been made to it since, and are daily making; several of which are related in the Philosophical Transactions. The best account of it, its various improvements and uses, is, I think, in Dr. Desaguliers's course of experimental philosophy, vol. II.

And, ready for the vacant space,
Incumbent Air resumes his place,
Depressing with stupendous force
Whate'er resists his downward course, 130
Pumps moved by rods from ponderous beams
Arrest the unsuspecting streams,
Which soon a sluggish pool would lie;
Then spout them foaming to the sky.

 Sagacious Savery! Taught by thee 135
Discordant elements agree,
Fire, water, air, heat, cold unite,
And listed in one service fight,
Pure streams to thirsty cities send,
Or deepest mines from floods defend. 140
Man's richest gift thy work will shine;
Rome's aqueducts were poor to thine!

At

[13]

At last the long descent is o'er;
Above your heads the billows roar:
High o'er your heads they roar in vain; 145
Not all the surges of the main
The dark recess can e're disclose,
Rocks heap'd on rocks th' attempt oppose:
Thrice Dover's cliff from you the tides
With interposing roof divides! 150

From such abyss restor'd to light,
Invade no more the realms of night.
For heroines it may well suffice
Once to have left these azure skies.

Above your heads, &c.] The mines are here sunk to the depth of one hundred and thirty fathoms, and are extended under the sea to places where there is, above them, sufficient depth of water for ships of large burden. These are the deepest coal-mines that have hitherto been wrought; and perhaps the miners have not in any other part of the globe, penetrated to so great a depth below the surface of the sea; the very deep mines in Hungary, Peru, and elsewhere, being situated in mountainous countries, where the surface of the earth is elevated to a great height above the level of the ocean.

Heroes

Heroes themselves, in days of yore, 155
Bold as they were, achiev'd no more.
Without a dread descent you may
The mines in their effects survey,
And with an easy eye look down
On that fair port and happy town. 160

Where late along the naked strand,
The fisher's cot did lonely stand,
And his poor bark unshelter'd lay,
Of every swelling surge the prey,
Now lofty piers their arms extend, 165
And with their strong embraces bend
Round crowded fleets, which safe defy
All storms that rend the wintry sky,
And bulwarks beyond bulwarks chain
The fury of the roaring main. 170
The peopl'd vale fair dwellings fill,
And lengthening streets ascend the hill;

Where

Where Industry intent to thrive,
Brings all her honey to the hive,
Religion strikes with reverent awe,   175
Example works th' effect of law,
And Plenty's flowing cup we see
Untainted yet by Luxury.

  THESE are the glories of the mine!
Creative Commerce, these are thine!   180

The glories of the mine, &c.] These mines were first wrought, for foreign consumption, by Sir John Lowther, Bart. one of the Lords of the Admiralty in the reign of King William; a person of great abilities, and a generous benefactor to his native country; who, by the encouragements which he gave to tradesmen and artificers of all kinds to settle at Whitehaven, may be esteemed the founder of that town. His son and successor, Sir James Lowther, pursuing the same plan, has brought these mines to their present state of perfection. It has been computed, that these two gentlemen, in the compass of a century (which time they have enjoyed these mines) have expended in one of them only upwards of half a million sterling.—The money returned hither for coals exported hence, greatly contributes to enable this remote country to pay those large sums, that are continually drained out of it in taxes and customs, in rents to absentees, and for clothing and various other necessary commodities, which those parts do not afford.—By this trade, and its consequences, the town of Whitehaven has been raised, from very low beginnings, to its present state; the country round it improved; and great numbers of hardy sailors, and other useful artificers trained up to serve their King and country in the navy, as well as in the home and foreign trades of the kingdom.

               HERE

Here while delighted you impart
Delight to every eye and heart,
Behold, grown jealous of your stay,
Your native Stream his charms display,
To court you to his banks again;   185
Now wind in wanton waves his train,
Now spread into a chrystal plain;
Then hid by pendent rocks would steal,
But tuneful Falls his course reveal,
As down the bending vale he roves   190
Thro' Yanwath woods, and Buckholme's groves;
Whose broad o'erspreading boughs beneath
Warbling he flows, while Zephyrs breathe.

 Here softly swells the spacious lawn,
Where bounds the buck, and skips the fawn, 200

 Your native stream, &c.] The river Lowther.
 Then hid by pendent rocks, &c.] See, in Mr. Dalton's Drawings, a view of this river near the bridge and church of Askham.
 As down the bending vale, &c.] See his view (taken from Clifton) of the river winding between Yanwath and Buckholme woods round the Elysian fields.
 Here softly swells, &c.] See his view, on a small scale, taken from Askham-

There

Or, couch'd beneath the hawthorn-trees,
In dappled groupes enjoy the breeze.

AMID yon sunny plain, alone,
To patriarchal rev'rence grown,
An oak for many an age has stood   205
Himself a widely waving wood,
While men and herds, with swift decay,
Race after race, have pass'd away.
See still his central trunk sustain
Huge boughs, which round o'erhang the plain,   210
And hospitable shade inclose,
Where flocks and herds at ease repose!

THERE the brown fells ascend the sky,
Below, the green inclosures lye;
Along their sloping sides supine   215
The peaceful villages recline:

fell, of the situation of Lowther-hall, park, &c. terminated by a long range of very high mountains, called Cross-fell.

On azure roofs bright sun-beams play,
And make the meanest dwelling gay.
Thus oft the wise all-ruling mind
Is to the lowly cottage kind, 220
Bids there His beams of favour fall,
While sorrow clouds the lofty hall,
That This may fear his awful frown,
And grateful That his goodness own.

If, grown familiar to the sight, 225
Lowther itself should less delight,
Then change the scene: To nature's pride,
Sweet Keswick's vale, the muse will guide.
The muse, who trod th' inchanted ground,
Who sail'd the wondrous lake around, 230
With you will haste once more to hail
The beauteous brook of Borrodale.

On azure roofs, &c.] The houses of this country are covered with a beautiful blue slate.

From

From savage parent gentle stream!
Be thou the Muse's favourite theme:
O soft infinuating glide   235
Silent along the meadow's side,
Smooth o'er the sandy bottom pass,
Resplendent all thro' fluid glass,
Unless upon thy yielding breast
Their painted heads the lillies rest,   240
To where in deep capacious bed
The widely liquid lake is spread.

Let other streams rejoyce to roar
Down the rough rocks of dread Lodore,
Rush raving on with boisterous sweep,   245
And foaming rend the frighted deep,
Thy gentle Genius shrinks away
From such a rude unequal fray;

Of dread Lodore, &c.] A very high cascade here falls into the lake of Derwent-water, near where Borrodale-beck (or brook) enters into it, as is described above.

Thro' thine own native dale, where rife
Tremendous rocks amid the fkies, 250
Thy waves with patience flowly wind,
Till they the fmootheft channel find,
Soften the horrors of the fcene,
And thro' confufion flow ferene.

 HORRORS like thefe at firft alarm, 255
But foon with favage grandeur charm
And raife to nobleft thought the mind:
Thus by thy fall, Lodore, reclin'd,
The craggy cliff, impendent wood,
Whofe fhadows mix o'er half the flood, 260
The gloomy clouds, which folemn fail,
Scarce lifted by the languid gale
O'er the cap'd hill, and darken'd vale;
The ravening kite, and bird of Jove,
Which round th' aerial ocean rove, 265
And, floating on the billowy fky,
With full expanded pennons fly,

Their

Their flutt'ring or their bleating prey
Thence with death-dooming eye survey;
Channels by rocky torrents torn,   270
Rocks to the lake in thunder born,
Or such as o'er our heads appear
Suspended in their mid career,
To start again at His command,
Who rules fire, water, air, and land,   275
I view with wonder and delight,
A pleasing, tho' an awful sight:
For, seen with them, the verdant Isles
Soften with more delicious smiles,
More tempting twine their opening bowers,   280
More lively glow the purple flowers,
More smoothly slopes the border gay,
In fairer circle bends the bay,

Channels by rocky torrents torn, &c.] For an account of an extraordinary storm in a part of this country, called St. John's Vale, by which numerous fragments of rocks were driven down from the mountains, along with cataracts of water, see a letter from Cockermouth, inserted in the Gentleman's Magazine of October, 1754.

And

And laſt, to fix our wand'ring eyes,
Thy roofs, O Keſwick, brighter riſe   285
The lake and lofty hills between,
Where Giant Skiddow ſhuts the ſcene.

Supreme of mountains, Skiddow, hail!
To whom all Britain ſinks a vale!
Lo, his imperial brow I ſee   290
From foul uſurping vapours free!
'Twere glorious now his ſide to climb,
Boldly to ſcale his top ſublime,
And thence—My muſe, theſe flights forbear,
Nor with wild raptures tire the fair.   295
Hills, rocks, and dales have been too long
The ſubject of thy rambling ſong.

Where Giant Skiddow, &c.] With the above-mentioned Drawings the curious reader may ſee three different Views of this beautiful lake, all exactly copied after nature. The firſt, of the whole lake, taken from Lodore, and terminated by Skiddow. The ſecond, taken from the parſonage-houſe, and terminated by Borrodale. The third, from Hill-top, with Caſlow-cragg appearing on the fore-ground; and alſo One of the caſcade.

Far

Far other scenes Their minds employ,
And move their hearts with softer joy.
For pleasures They need never roam, 300
Theirs with affection dwell, at home.
Thrice happy They at home to prove
A Parent's and a Brother's love,
Her bright example pleas'd to trace,
Learn every virtue every grace, 305
Which lustre give in female life
To daughter, sister, parent, wife;
Grateful to see her guardian care
A tender father's loss repair,
And, rising far o'er grief and pain, 310
The glories of her race maintain.

THEIR antient seats let others fly
To strole beneath a foreign sky,
Or loytering in their villas stay,
Till useless summers waste away, 315

While, hopeless of their lords' return,
The poor exhausted tenants mourn;
From Lowther She disdains to run
To bask beneath a southern sun,
Opens the hospitable door, 320
Welcomes the friend, relieves the poor;
Bids tenants share the lib'ral board,
And early know and love their lord,
Whose courteous deeds to all extend,
And make each happy guest a friend. 325
To smiling Earth the grateful Main
Thus gives her gather'd streams again
In showers on hill and dale and plain.

O may the virtues, which adorn
With modest beams his rising morn, 330
Unclouded grow to perfect day!
May He with bounty's brightest ray

The

The natives chear, enrich the soil,

With arts improve, reward their toil,

Glad with kind warmth our northern sky,

And generous Lonsdale's loss supply. 335

—*enrich the soil* &c.] The late Lord Lonsdale spared no expence of money or time to introduce woollen and linen Manufactures into the county of Westmoreland; to improve the natives in the art of husbandry by his own example, and encourage them by suitable rewards. Besides conferring premiums on those who excell'd, he also, in order to conquer the force of ignorance and prejudice, more obstinate perhaps than the soil, apprenticed out into neighbouring counties, which were more skilled in agriculture, several sons of his tenants for that laudable purpose; and laid them under obligation to return again, and exercise that Art, for a certain term, in their own country.

HERE the Author thinks himself bound to acknowledge, that he owes the Explanatory Notes, on the description of the mines, to Dr. Brownrigg of Whitehaven.—The kind and friendly design with which they were sent to him, will best appear from the letter which accompany'd them; and which is here subjoined. If the inquisitive reader should desire to see a larger specimen of that Gentleman's knowledge of philosophical and commercial subjects, he would recommend him to a treatise entituled, " The art of making Common Salt, as now practised in " most parts of the world; with several Improvements proposed in that art, for the " use of the British dominions; by William Brownrigg, M. D. and F. R. S." but that it is now, he believes, out of print. However he may have his curiosity in some degree gratified, by a good account of that work, given by Mr. Watson in the Philosophical Transactions, N° 487, for the months of April, May, and part of June, 1748.

E *A* LET-

A LETTER to the AUTHOR.

SIR,

I Give you thanks for the pleasure I have received in the perusal of your poem, heightened perhaps by a fondness for every thing that you have there so elegantly described. I am however apprehensive, that such of your readers as are unacquainted with your subject, may not have the same relish for several parts of your peformance. Much of the pleasure which we receive from descriptions of the country must arise from recalling to mind those rural scenes that have given us delight, and from comparing them with their representations; and observing with what art and judgment those representations are copied after nature. And altho' the scenes delineated in your poetic landskips, seem as beautifully varied, and as well adapted to give pleasure to the judicious as those that are most admired in other countries, and may serve as excellent models for the embellishment of rural situations: yet, it must be owned that, in this part of your poem, you labour under some disadvantage, from the choice of your subject in a retired part; which does not fall so much under the eye of the curious as Windsor Forest and some other places, whose charms have been displayed by some of our best poets. However, very happily for you, though your Brother has devoted the largest share of his time and study this summer to the adorning our New Church with his Painting, yet he has found leisure to make very exact Drawings of the places you describe. These, as they are the best comment on this part of your work, will, I hope, in a great measure remove the difficulty here hinted at; and the Public will have the pleasure of seeing the sister arts mutually reflecting light upon each other, and conspiring, by a friendly emulation, to set off these beautiful scenes to the best advantage.

Another part of your performance will, I am afraid, be attended with greater difficulties. Your descriptions of the country must be generally understood; and, like a fine picture, will be admired by many who do not know the original; although they will be read with most delight by those who are best acquainted with your subject. But few of your readers will have such a knowledge of mines as will enable them to follow you through their dark and intricate labyrinths. More especially, as these are a subject that has not, I think, before been attempted in verse. And yet they seem well to deserve the notice of our poets, as they

they abound in objects proper to excite admiration, and are one great source of the wealth and power of these kingdoms. Here it may be worth the while to stop a little, and reflect on the labour and dangers that They sustain, who, from the mines, supply us with many necessaries and conveniencies of life: what multitudes of people by them are maintained: what efforts of human reason are there exerted, in the most ingenious inventions: and what immense treasures are thence raised, by which numberless wheels are set on motion in the complicated machine of commerce. The subterranean regions, hitherto delineated by the luxuriant fancies of poets, are widely different from these great funds of treasure. And as the veracity of those poets, who have descended into the lower regions, hath often been called in question, some may even suspect that you also have indulged yourself in this poetic licence, and have related such things of these dark abodes as would best appear in verse, rather than as you really found them in nature. To obviate which suspicions, may it not be necessary to produce authentic vouchers of your having faithfully described such objects as occured to you in the coal-mines? Had Cervantes taken this method, his wonderful account of a certain cave would perhaps have met with more credit than it now does, notwithstanding his artful insinuation of its having been believed by a very great scholar. The Explanatory Notes, which, agreeable to your request, I send inclosed, and which you are at liberty to publish with your poem, may serve as a sort of circumstantial proof of the truth of your descriptions. You will readily perceive that the nature of your design would not allow me to write an history of collieries, or a philosophical dissertation on damps. I have therefore contented myself with relating a few facts which may throw some light on this part of your poem, and may help to render your description of the mines intelligible to your readers.

I am, &c.

Whitehaven,
Nov. 20, 1754.

W. BROWNRIGG.

SOME THOUHGTS
ON
BUILDING and PLANTING,
TO
Sir JAMES LOWTHER,
Of LOWTHER-HALL, Bart.

TO
Sir JAMES LOWTHER, Bart.

HEN stately structures Lowther grace,
Worthy the Owner and the Place,
Fashion will not the works direct,
But Reason be the architect.

READY each beauteous Order stands   5
To execute what She commands.
The Doric grave, where weight requires,
To give his manly strength aspires;

The Doric grave, where weight requires.] In ea æde cum voluissent columnas collocare, non habentes symmetrias earum, & quærentes quibus rationibus efficere pos-

The

The light Corinthian, richly gay,

Does all embellishments display; 10

Between them see, with matron air,

Th' Ionic, delicately fair!

THESE their abundant aid will lend

To answer every structure's end.

To Building can a mode belong 15

But Gay, or Delicate, or Strong?

sent, ut & *ad onus ferendum* essent idoneæ, & in aspectu probatam haberent venustatem : dimensi sunt virilis pedis vestigium, & cum invenissent pedem sextam partem esse altitudinis in homine, ita in columnam transtulerunt : & qua crassitudine fecerunt basin scapi, tantum eam sexies cum capitulo in altitudinem extulerunt. Ita Dorica columna *virilis corporis* proportionem, & firmitatem & venustatem in ædificiis præstare cœpit. *Vitruv.* L. IV. C. i. p. 60.

The light Corinthian, &c.] Tertium vero, quod Corinthium dicitur, virginalis habet gracilitatis imitationem : quod virgines propter ætatis teneritatem gracilioribus membris figuratæ, effectus recipiunt in ornatu venustiores. Ejus autem capituli prima inventio, &c. Ibid.

Between them see, &c.] Junoni, Dianæ, Libero Patri, cæterisq; Diis qui eadem sunt similitudine, si ædes Ionicæ construerentur, habita erit ratio *mediocritatis*, quod & ab severo more Doricorum & a teneritate Corinthiorum, temperabitur earum institutio proprietatis. *Ibid.*

Th' Ionic, &c.] Item postea Dianæ constituere ædem quærentes, novi generis speciem, iisdem vestigiis ad muliebrem transtulerunt gracilitatem : & fecerunt primum columnæ crassitudinem altitudinis octava parte : ut haberent speciem excelsiorem, basi spiram supposuerunt pro calceo, capitulo volutas, uti capillamento concrispatos cincinnos præpendentes dextra ac sinistra collocaverunt, & cymatiis & encarpis pro crinibus dispositis, frontes ornaverunt : truncoq; toto strias, uti stolarum rugas, *matronali more* dimiserunt. *Ibid.*

Why

Why search we then for Orders new,
Rich in these all-comprising few,
But that the standard rules of Greece
Disdain to humour wild caprice? 20
They Fancy's wanton freaks controul,
In every part consult the whole,
Teach art to dress, and not disguise,
Seek lasting fame, not short surprise,
And all Adornings to produce 25
From real or from seeming Use,
The Place's Genius to revere,
And, as He bids, the structure rear.

   SMILES He o'er fragrant Flora's bloom?
Ne'er shock him with a grotto's gloom. 30

———*from real or from seeming use*] ——quemadmodum mutuli cantheriorum projecturæ ferunt *imaginem*, sic in Ionicis denticuli ex projecturis asserum habent imitationem. Itaque in Græcis operibus nemo sub mutulo denticulos constituit: non enim possunt subtus cantherios asseres esse. Quod ergo supra cantherios & templa in *veritate* debet esse collocatum, id in *imaginibus*, si infra constitutum fuerit, mendosam habebit operis rationem; &c.

Nor with smooth slender columns mock
His roughness in the rugged rock.
Nor by trim steps hand gently down
(Like dainty dames in formal town)
The nimble Naiades, who bound   35
O'er native rocks with sprightly sound.
Nor roving Dryades confine
Precisely to a single line,
Streight, circular, or serpentine.

ALL forms arise at Nature's call,   40
And Use can beauty give to all.
None e're disgust the judging mind,
When vary'd well, or well combin'd.

THIS Lowther's Noble Planter knew,
And kept it in his constant view.   45
So sweetly wild his woods are strown,
Nature mistakes them for her own,

Yet

Yet all to proper soil and site
So suited, doubly they delight.

While tender plants in vales repose, 50
Where the mild Zephyr only blows,
Embattled Firs bleak hills adorn,
Under whose safe-guard smiles the corn.
Who builds or plants, this rule should know,
FROM TRUTH AND USE ALL BEAUTIES FLOW. 55

From Truth, &c.] ――――quod non potest in *veritate* fieri, id non putaverunt in imaginibus factum, posse certam rationem habere. Omnia enim certa proprietate, & a *veris naturæ* deductis moribus, traduxerunt in operum perfectiones: & ea probaverunt, quorum explicationes in disputationibus rationem possunt habere *veritatis.* Vitruv. Lib. IV. C. ii. p. 67. Edit. de Læt.

――――*and Use,* &c.] See the Idea of Beauty explained by the great Dr. Berkley in the Minute Philosoqher, Dial. III. Sect. viii, ix. Edit. 3. 1752.

F I N I S.

To be had of J. and J. RIVINGTON, *at the Bible and Crown in St. Paul's Church-yard, and of* R. and J. DODSLEY, *at Tully's Head in Pall-Mall.*

TWO Epistles, written A. D. 1735 and 1744.

Three Sermons preached before the University of Oxford at St. Mary's on September 15, and October 20, 1745, and November 5, 1747.

A Sermon preached at the Abbey Church at Bath, December. 8, 1745.

A Sermon preached before the Right Honourable the Earl of Northumberland, President, and the Governors of the Middlesex Hospital, at St Ann's Westminster, April 1751.

By JOHN DALTON, D.D.

Shortly will be published, the Second Edition *of*

Remarks on Twelve Historical Designs of Raphael, and the Musæum Græcum & Ægyptiacum, or, Antiquities and Views of Greece and Egypt, illustrated by Prints from Mr. Dalton's *Drawings.* To which Remarks is now added, by another Hand, An Essay on the *Six Prints* from Raphael.

NOTES to *A Descriptive Poem*

p. 101. '*his native country*': Cumberland and Westmorland. Dalton, who spent most of his adulthood in London and the Midlands of England, is using the word country as a synonym for region.

'*by the Poet*': Claudian (Claudius Claudianus, c.370–c.404), an eminent poet of late Roman antiquity. The description to which Dalton refers is from *De raptu Proserpinae*, an unfinished epic poem known to English audiences through, among other sources, Leonard Digges's translation *The Rape of Proserpina* (1617) and, in Dalton's lifetime, Jabez Hughes's translation in *The Rape of Proserpine, from Claudian. In Three Books* (London: F. Burleigh, 1714). The abduction of Proserpina (the Roman counterpart of the goddess Persephone) was also well known to English readers on account of Ovid's renditions of the myth in *Metamorphoses* (V.341–661) and *Fasti* (IV.417–620).

'*chariot of Ceres*': Dalton refers to the portrayal of the goddess Ceres (the Roman counterpart of the Greek goddess Demeter) in Claudian's *Rape of Proserpina*. Ceres was often depicted in such a manner; compare Ovid, *Metamorphoses* (V.642–47).

p. 102. '————*cano rota pulvere labens*', etc.: Claudian, *De raptu Proserpinae* (I.187–90). Compare Hughes's translation of 1714 (p. 15): 'The whirling Wheels, revolving o'er the Ground, | The Fields impregnate as the Glebe they wound. | A sudden Harvest starts upon the Plain, | And in their Footsteps springs the yellow Grain.'

'*The Mines*', etc.: See Introduction above, pp. 36–37, 45. It seems likely that Dalton's poem describes a tour of the workings at the Saltom pit (NX 964 173), which opened in 1729. See, indicatively, l. 26 on p. 111 and the footnote on p. 115.

'*two very amiable Persons*': presumably, two of the daughters of Robert and Katherine Lowther, and therefore the sisters of Sir James Lowther (1736–1802). See Introduction above, p. 24–25.

'*classical allusion and parody, &c.*': Parody in this context refers to the convention of applying the elevated style and conceits of classical poetry to either trivial or unconventional subjects. The success of Alexander Pope's mock-heroic poem *The Rape of the Lock* (1712–1717) affirms the fashionable interest in such works among Dalton's contemporaries. The extracts Dalton presents are from Claudian's *Rape of Proserpina* and from the works of Virgil (Publius Vergilius Maro, 70–19 BCE), the preeminent poet of Golden Age Latin literature. Dalton includes quotations from Virgil's epic *The Aeneid* and his *Georgics*. Both of these works exerted a profound influence on eighteenth-century English literature, not least on account of the translations published by John Dryden in *The Works of Virgil*, 3 vols. (London: J. Tonson, 1697).

'———————*quae te fortuna fatigat*', etc.: Virgil, *Aeneid* (VI.533–34). Compare Robert Fagles's translation in *The Aeneid* (London: Penguin Books, Ltd., 2006), p. 200, ll. 621–22: 'What destiny hounds you on to visit these, | these sunless homes of sorrow, harrowed lands?'

p. 103. '*At cantu commotae Erebi sedibus imis*', etc.: Virgil, *Georgics* (IV.471–72, 481–84). Compare C. Day Lewis's translation in Virgil: *The Eclogues, The Georgics* (Oxford: Oxford University Press, 1999), pp. 124–25: 'But, by his song aroused from Hell's nethermost basements, | Flocked out the flimsy shades, the phantoms lost to light | […] Why, Death's very home and holy of holies was shaken | To hear that song, and the Furies with steel-blue snakes entwined | In their tresses; the watch-dog Cerberus gaped open his triple mouth; | Ixion's wheel stopped dead from whirling in the wind.'

'*Nulla sit immunis regio, nullumque sub umbris*', etc.: Claudian, *De raptu Proserpinae* (I.225–28): 'Let no place be unburdened nor any sheltered breast be made inaccessible to Venus. Now let sorrowful Erinys* feel the flames of passion; let Acheron and the iron heart of solemn Dis be softened by love's wanton shafts.' *Erinys: one of the Furies, spirits of vengeance in classical Greek and Roman mythology.

'———————*divino semita gressu*', etc.: Claudian, *De raptu Proserpinae* (I.231–32): 'The path shone brightly beneath the divine steps.'

'*Hinc exaudiri gemitus, & saeva sonare*', etc.: Virgil, *Aeneid* (VI.557–58). Compare Fagles's translation (*Aeneid*, p. 200, ll. 647–48): 'Groans resound from the depths, the savage crack of the lash, the grating creak of iron, the clank of dragging chains.'

'*Hinc via Tartarii quae fert Acherontis ad undas—*', etc.: Virgil, *Aeneid* (VI.295–97). Compare Fagles's translation (*Aeneid*, p. 192, ll. 136–39): 'From there | the road leads down to the Acheron's Tartarean waves. | Here the enormous whirlpool gapes aswirl with filth, | seethes and spews out all its silt in the Wailing River.'

p. 104. '*the late Lord Lonsdale*': Henry Lowther, 4th Baronet of Lowther and 3rd Viscount Lonsdale (1694–1751). He distinguished himself for his loyalty to George I, and thus to the Protestant succession, during the Jacobite uprising of 1715. He served as Lord Lieutenant and Custos Rotulorum of Cumberland and Westmorland from 1738 until 1751, during which period he also established a factory for textile production in the buildings that had once comprised Lowther College. (See Owen, *The Lowther Family*, pp. 222–31.) After Henry's death, his baronetcy passed to his second cousin, James Lowther of Maulds Meaburn (1736–1802), who also inherited Henry's estates,

Notes to *A Descriptive Poem*

including Lowther Hall. It is to this James Lowther, who was created Earl of Lonsdale in 1784, that Dalton's poem on 'Building and Planting' is dedicated.

'present melancholy condition': The period between the end of the War of the Spanish Succession (1713) and the end of the Seven Years War (1763) was marked by the expansion of Britain's power overseas. At home, however, this period was also marked by economic depressions and increasing rates of poverty and destitution. During this half century the population of London is thought to have risen from somewhat more than half a million to nearly three-quarters of a million people: an 85% increase. See Clive Emsley, Tim Hitchcock, and Robert Shoemaker, *'*London History: London, 1715–1760*'*, *Old Bailey Proceedings Online* <www.oldbaileyonline.org> (06 May 2018).

'by a Noble Earl': presumably, Wills Hill, 1st Marquess of Downshire (1718–1793), who proposed a scheme for repealing and revising elements of the Poor Laws in England and Wales in 1752/53. See 'An Abstract of the Poor Bills', *London Magazine 21* (April 1752), pp. 153–54; and Richard Burn, *The History of the Poor Laws: With Observations* (London: A. Millar, 1764), pp. 192–95.

p. 105. *'some late violations'*: Dalton refers to the felling of the oak trees around Derwentwater, particularly at Crow Park, during the late 1740s and early 1750s. This event transformed the scenery around the lake. See Denman, *Materialising Cultural Value*, pp. 77–97.

'Where the rude axe with heaved stroke', etc.: Dalton is quoting John Milton's *Il Penseroso* (ll. 136–38). See Milton: *Complete Poems* p. 57. The extent of Milton's influence on eighteenth-century poetry cannot be overstated, and Dalton's poem contains several allusions and references to both Milton's epic *Paradise Lost* and to his lyric poems. See, R.D. Havens, *The Influence of Milton on English Poetry* (Cambridge, MA: Harvard University Press, 1922), pp. 236–75.

'The lonely mountains o'er', etc.: another quotation from Milton, *On the Morning of Christ's Nativity*, ll. 181–88. See Milton, *Complete Poems*, p. 24.,

p. 107. (l. 4) *'From sulphurous damps'*: like 'fulminating damps' or 'fire-damp', is a reference to methane gas. See 'damp, n.1', *Oxford English Dictionary Online* <www.oed.com> (06 May 2018). As J.V. Beckett has observed, methane leaks frequently 'killed and maimed men working underground' and were 'the single most important cause of death and injury in mines during the eighteenth century' (*Coal and Tobacco*, pp. 70–71). Flooding, as Dalton goes on to note, was also a hazard.

(l. 5) *'dire Aetnaen sound'*: Dalton refers to Mount Etna, a volcano in eastern Sicily which is archetypally associated with infernal powers in classical and canonical literature. See, indicatively, John Milton, *Paradise Lost*, ed. by

From the Mines to the Mountains

Alastair Fowler, 2nd edn (London: Routledge, 2013), p. 75 (I.230–37) and William Shakespeare, *Titus Andronicus*, ed. by Jonathan Bate (London: Routledge, 1995), p. 203 (III.1.242).

p. 108. *'Conceal'd till then from female sight?'*: The rationale for this statement is uncertain. There is no evidence to prove that the Lowther's daughters were the first women to tour the mines at Whitehaven.

p. 109. *(l. 23) 'young Ammon'*: Alexander the Great (356–323 BC), who visited the oracle of Ammon Ra in the Siwa Oasis in 331 BC and thereafter proclaimed himself the son of Jupiter Ammon. Compare Alexander Pope, *An Essay on Man: Epistle I* (l. 160), in *The Poems of Alexander Pope*, ed. by John Butt (New Haven, CT: Yale University Press, 1963)

(l. 25) *'sage Prospero'*: Carlisle Spedding (1695–1755), here styled as the legendary enchanter of Shakespeare's *The Tempest*, served as the steward of the Lowther family's collieries from 1730 until his death. During this time, Spedding oversaw the expansion and intensification of excavations around the West Cumberland coalfields, and he helped to introduce new measures to improve the safety of working conditions; the ventilation system to which Dalton refers in ll. 37–44 is a case in point. (See Beckett, *Coal and Tobacco*, pp. 72–73.)

p. 110. (ll. 35–36) *'kindred furies sung ... Orcus rung'*: Orcus, Roman god of the Underworld and counterpart of the Greek god Hades. Virgil describes the Furies (the spirits of vengeance) as having been born with Orcus in *Georgics* (I.277–78). See C. Day Lewis, *Virgil*, p. 60, and Hesiod, *Works and Days* (ll. 802–4), in *Theogony and Works and Days*, ed. by M.L. West (Oxford: Oxford University Press, 2000), p. 61.

(ll. 37–44) *'Tho' boiling with vain rage they sit'*, etc.: Dalton is describing the ventilation systems introduced by Spedding. See Beckett, *Coal and Tobacco*, pp. 72–73.

p. 111. (ll. 55–60) *'Nor strikes the flint, nor whirls the steel'*, etc.: Dalton is referring to the 'flint and steel' safety lantern devised by Carlisle Spedding. (See Beckett, *Coal and Tobacco*, pp. 71–72.) This invention captured the interest of several eighteenth-century visitors to Whitehaven. See, for example, Donaldson, et al., *Hobhouse's Tour*, pp. 17, 42.

p. 112. (l. 60) *'grisly'*: meaning, grim or ghastly. See 'grisly, adj.', *Oxford Englis Dictionary Online* <www.oed.com> (accessed 5 June 2018).

(l. 62) *'Tartarian tempests'*: an allusion to Tartarus, the deepest part of the underworld in classical mythology. In the *Aeneid* (VI.577), Virgil portrays the region as being twice as far below the earth as Hades.

(l.64) *'great Stygian holiday'*: an allusion to the River Styx, the boundary between the Earth and the Underworld in classical mythology.

Notes to *A Descriptive Poem*

(l. 67) *'Aetheopian teeth'*: the idea is that the collier's teeth appear even more white on account of his swarthy complexion. The conceit would seem to derive from a logical proposition which appears in (among other places) Duns Scotus, *Ordinatio* (III.11.2). See Richard Cross, *The Metaphysics of the Incarnation: Thomas Aquinas to Duns Scotus* (Oxford: Oxford University Press, 2002), pp. 203–4.

(l. 68) *'"Grin horrible a ghastly smile"'*: a near quotation of Milton's description of Death in *Paradise Lost* (II.845–47): 'and Death | Grinned horrible a ghastly smile, to hear | His famine should be filled'. See Milton *Paradise Lost*, p. 151(ll. 72-76)

(ll. 72–76) *'Of gloomy Dis, infernal god … eternal pains'*: Dalton is alluding to the descent of the poet and minstrel Orpheus into the Underworld to retrieve his deceased wife, Eurydice. (Compare Virgil, *Georgics,* IV.453–527, to which Dalton referred on p. v.) Dis, the god of death, is the Roman counterpart of the Greek god Hades.

p. 113. (ll. 81–86) *'The with increasing wonder gaze'*, etc.: Dalton's description of the inner workings of the pits is reminiscent of descriptions of the city of Underworld in classical literature, including Milton's description of 'Pandaemonium' in *Paradise Lost* (I.697ff.).

p. 114. (l. 90) *'Thick Acherontic rivers roll'*: Acheron (literally, 'the river of woe'), the principal river of the Underworld in classical Greek and Roman mythology. See, indicatively, Virgil, *Aeneid* (VI.295–97), one of the extracts Dalton quotes on p. v.

(l. 93) *'wing'd Zephyrs resort'*: Zephyr, the west wind in classical mythology and by association any gentle wind or breeze. Hence, John Milton's *L'Allegro* (ll. 18–19): 'The frolick Wind that breathes the spring, | Zephir with *Aurora* playing'. See Milton, *Complete Poems,* p. 48.

(l. 94) *'Infernal Darkness'*: presumably a rendering of the Latin 'infernae tenebrae'. See Virgil, *Aeneid* (VII, 323–26).

(l. 98) *'cordials'*: reviving draughts of air. The word cordials is used in accordance with definition 2.a. in the *Oxford English Dictionary*: 'Stimulating, "comforting", or invigorating the heart'. See 'cordial, adj. and n.', *Oxford English Dictionary Online* <www.oed.com> (06 May 2018). Dalton's turn of phrase recalls Pope's translation of *The Odyssey* (IV.600).

p. 115. (l. 101) *'the wondering muse'*: Dalton refers here less to one of the Muses (the nine goddesses of the arts and sciences in classical Greek and Roman mythology), than to his own awe-struck poetic imagination. Such an abstract notion of the term muse was prevalent in the poetry of this period.

(l. 105) *'by the nitrous blast'*: by gun-powder, which was used for blasting at the Lowther's collieries from as early as 1717. See Beckett, *Coal and*

From the Mines to the Mountains

Tobacco, p. 68.

pp. 116–17. (ll.121–34) *'High on hug axis heav'd, above,'* etc.: Dalton is describing the Newcomen steam engines (or 'fire-engines') that were employed at the Lowther's collieries from 1715. See Beckett, *Coal and Tobacco*, 68–71, and Allen, 'Newcomen Engines at Whitehaven'.

Footnote: *'While pent within the iron womb'*: *&c.:* A description and diagram of Thomas Savery's steam engine appears in the entry for 'Engine' in John Harris's *Lexicon Technicum: Or, An Universal English Dictionary of Arts and Sciences* (London: D. Brown, et al., 1704). The note also refers to John Theophilus Desaguliers (1683–1744) and his Course of Experimental Philosophy, Vol. 2 (London: W. Innys, et al., 1744), pp. 464–90.

p. 118. (l. 135) *'Sagacious Savery!'*: Thomas Savery (c.1650–1715), the inventor of the first commercially used steam engine in England (patented in 1698). Dalton's declaration is somewhat misleading. As his own descriptions make clear, it was Thomas Newcomen (1664–1729)'s engines that were employed in the Lowther's collieries. Newcomen's engines (first manufactured in 1712) improved on some of the limitations of Savery's original design. See Allen, 'Newcomen Engines at Whitehaven'.

p. 119. (l. 149) *'Thrice Dover's cliff from you the tides'*, etc.: The depth of the Saltom pit was closer to 80 fathoms. It is not clear where Brownrigg got the measurement of 130 fathoms. The Cliffs of Dover reach as high as 110 m, so the estimation given in Dalton's poem is also exaggerated.

p. 120. (ll. 155–56) *'Heroes themselves, in days of yore,'* etc.: a reference to journeys into the Underworld in classical Greek and Roman mythology, such as the one portrayed by Virgil in *Book VI* of the *Aeneid*.

(ll. 160–78) *'Where late along the naked strand,'* etc.: Dalton's imaginative vision of the development of Whitehaven is not wholly fanciful. The town expanded substantially as a site of industry and commerce between the late seventeenth century and the mid-eighteenth century. See Beckett, *Coal and Tobacco*, and Collier and Pearson, *Whitehaven 1660–1800.*.

p. 121. Footnote: *'The glories of the mine, &c.'*: Sir John Lowther (1642–1706), 2nd Baronet of Whitehaven, was born at Whitehaven and played a pivotal role in the development and expansion of the town during the latter seventeenth century. He served as MP for Cumberland from 1665 until 1700, and as Lord Commissioner of the Admiralty between 1689 and 1696. See Owen, *The Lowther Family*, pp. 240–45, 248–54

p. 122. (l. 184) *'Your native Stream'*: the Lowther, which flows near Lowther Hall, the ancestral country seat of the two ladies' brother, Sir James Lowther (1736–1802), from 1751.

(l. 191) *'Thro' Yanwath woods, and Buckholme's groves'*: Yanwath (NY 510 727) descended to the earls of Lonsdale in the mid-seventeenth century. Buckholme Wood (NY 526 252), near Lowther Hall, came into the family's possession during the early fifteenth century.

Footnote: 'Then hid by pendent rocks, &c.': The Mr Dalton mentioned in the footnotes is Dalton's brother Richard (c.1715–1791), one of the foremost illustrators of antiquities of the era. The editors have not been able to determine whether copies of these drawing of local scenes still exist. John and Richard Dalton had collaborated previously; see Dalton's *Remarks on Twelve Historical Designs of Raphael, and the Museum Graecum et Egytiacum* (1752), the second edition of which is advertised at the back of *Descriptive Poem*. The Askham (NY 512 923) referred to lies adjacent to Lowther Hall and came into the possession of the Lowther family during the late seventeenth century.

Footnote: 'As down the bending vale, &c.: The 'Elysian fields' would appear to be a reference to the grounds of the estate of Lowther Hall.

p. 124. (l. 230) '*the wonderous lake*': Derwent Water (NY 260 210).

(l. 232) '*The beauteous brook of Borrodale*': the River Derwent, which enters Derwent Water near NY 263 193.

p. 125. (l. 235) '*insinuating*': the word is here used literally to refer to the sinuous winding of the river. See 'insinuating, adj.', *Oxford English Dictionary Online* <www.oed.com> (06 May 2018).

(l. 244) '*Let other streams rejoice to roar*': Watendlath Beck, which forms Lodore Falls (NY 264 187).

(l. 247) '*gentle Genius*': gentle character. The word genius is used in accordance with definition II.a. in the *Oxford English Dictionary*. See 'genius, n. and adj.', *Oxford English Dictionary Online* <www.oed.com> (accessed 5 June 2018).

p. 126. (ll. 255–57) '*Horrors like these at first alarm*', etc.: Such a conception of horror accords with the principles advanced by Joseph Addison's influential essays on the 'Pleasures of the Imagination' (1712), and with Edmund Burke's later characterisation of the sublime as denoting entities whose incomprehensibility both overawes and exhilarates the imagination. See Joseph Addison, *The Spectator*, 418 (30 June 1712), n.p., and Edmund Burke, *Philosophical Enquiry*, pp. 41–72.

(l.264) '*The ravening kite, and bird of Jove*': the ravenous eagle, the bird associated with the Roman god Jupiter (or Jove), counterpart of the Greek god Zeus. Ravening, like ravenous, derives from the classical Latin *rapina* ('robbery'). See 'ravine, n.1 and adj.', *Oxford English Dictionary Online* <www.oed.com> (accessed 5 June 2018)

From the Mines to the Mountains

p. 127. Footnote : *'Channels by rocky torrents torn &.')*: Dalton refers to Smith, 'Dreadful Storm in Cumberland'.

p. 128. (l. 288–89) *'Supreme of mountains, Skiddow, hail!'*, etc.: Dalton is mistaken about the supremacy of Skiddaw, which is only the 3rd highest mountain in England. The idea that Skiddaw was England's highest mountain had been perpetuated by William Camden's *Britannia* from the 5th edition of 1600. By the 1720s, however, commentators including Daniel Defoe had begun to disabuse readers of this misconception. See William Camden, *Britannia*, 5th edn (London: G. Bishop, 1600), 692–93, and Daniel Defoe, *A Tour thro' the Whole Island of Great Britain, Divided into Circuits or Journies*, 3 vols. (London: G. Strahan, 1727), III, p. 231.

p. 129. (l. 301) *'A Parent's and a Brother's love'*: The reference is to the two ladies' mother, Katherine Lowther (1712–1764), and their brother Sir James. Their father Robert Lowther (1681–1745) had been deceased for nearly a decade when Dalton composed his poem.

p. 130. (l. 316) *'hopeless of their lords' return'*: Henry Lowther, 4th Baronet of Lowther and 3rd Viscount Lonsdale (1694–1751).

p. 131. (l. 335) *'generous Lonsdale's loss'*: A further reference to Henry Lowther, then recently deceased. As noted above, he established a factory for textile production in the buildings that had once comprised Lowther College.

'Mr. Watson in the Philosophical Transactions': Dalton refers to 'An Account of a Treatise by Wm. Brownrigg M.D. F.R.S. intituled, "The Art of making common salt, as now practised in most parts of the world; with several improvements proposed in that art, for the use of the British dominions;" abstracted by W. Watson F.R.S.', *Philosphical Transactions* 45, (1748), pp. 351–72.

p. 132. *'your Brother'*: Richard Dalton (c.1715–1791), who painted the altar at St James' Church during 1754.

'as these are a subject that has not, I think, before been attempted in verse': Brownrigg presumably did not know of Thomas Yalden's 'To Sir Humphry Mackworth: On the Mines, Late of Sir Carbery Price' (1710) or of James Weeks's *Poetical Prospects of Workington and Whitehaven* (1752). He is nonetheless correct to call attention to the relative novelty of the subject matter of Dalton's poem.

p. 133. *'Cervantes'*: Miguel de Cervantes Saavedra (1547–1616); Brownrigg is referring to the account of the Cave of Montesinos in the second part of Cervantes's *Don Quixote* (1615).

p. 135.

'To Sir James Lowther, Bart.': Sir James Lowther (1736–1802).

Notes to *A Descriptive Poem*

Footnote: '*The Doric grave, where weight requires*': Dalton is quoting from Vitruvius Pollio's *De Architectura* (IV.1.6). See Vitruvius, *The Ten Books on Architecture*, trans. by Morris Hicky Morgan (Cambridge, MA: Harvard University Press, 1914), p. 103: 'Wishing to set up columns in that temple, but not having rules for their symmetry, and being in search of some way by which they could render them fit to bear a load and also of a satisfactory beauty of appearance, they measured the imprint of a man's foot and compared this with his height. On finding that, in a man, the foot was one sixth of the height, they applied the same principle to the column, and reared the shaft, including the capital, to a height six times its thickness at its base. Thus the Doric column, as used in buildings, began to exhibit the proportions, strength, and beauty of the body of a man.'

p. 136. Footnote: '*The light Corinthian, &c.*': *De Architectura* (IV.1.8); Vitruvius, *Ten Books*, p. 104: 'The third order, called Corinthian, is an imitation of the slenderness of a maiden; for the outlines and limbs of maidens, being more slender on account of their tender years, admit of prettier effects in the way of adornment.'

Footnote: '*Between them see, &c.*': *De Architectura* (I.2.5); Vitruvius, *Ten Books*, p. 15: 'The construction of temples of the Ionic order to Juno, Diana, Father Bacchus, and the other gods of that kind, will be in keeping with the middle position which they hold; for the building of such will be an appropriate combination of the severity of the Doric and the delicacy of the Corinthian.'

Footnote: '*Th' Ionic, &c.*': *De Architectura* (IV.1.7); Vitruvius, *Ten Books*, pp. 103–4: 'Just so afterwards, when they desired to construct a temple to Diana in a new style of beauty, they translated these footprints into terms characteristic of the slenderness of women, and thus first made a column the thickness of which was only one eighth of its height, so that it might have a taller look. At the foot they substituted the base in place of a shoe; in the capital they placed the volutes, hanging down at the right and left like curly ringlets, and ornamented its front with cymatia and with festoons of fruit arranged in place of hair, while they brought the flutes down the whole shaft, falling like the folds in the robes worn by matrons.'

p. 137 (l. 27): '*The Place's Genius*', etc.: As above, genius here refers to the character or essential quality of the place.

(l. 29): '*fragrant Flora's bloom*': Flora, counterpart of the Ancient Greek goddess Chloris, is the Roman goddess of flowers and the spring.

Footnote: '*—from real or from seeming use*': *De Architectura* (IV.2.5); Vitruvius, *Ten Books*, pp. 108–9: 'Just as mutules represent the projection of the principal rafters, so dentils in the Ionic are an imitation of the projections of the common rafters. And so in Greek works nobody ever put dentils under mutules, as it is impossible that common rafters should be underneath principal rafters. Therefore, if that which in the original must be placed above the principal rafters, is put in the copy below them, the result will be a work constructed on false principles.'

p. 138. (l. 35): *'The nimble Naiades'*: In classical mythology the naiads are nymphs who preside over waterways, including brooks, streams, and springs. They are also often associated with fountains and wells.

(l. 37): *'roving Dryades'*: In classical mythology, dyrads are tree nymphs. Conventionally associated with the oak (Greek, *drûs*), dryads can be associated with trees in general.

p. 139. Footnote: *'From Truth, &c.'*: *De Architectura* (IV.2.5–6); Vitruvius, *Ten Books*, p. 109: 'the ancients held that what could not happen in the original would have no valid reason for existence in the copy. For in all their works they proceeded on definite principles of fitness and in ways derived from the truth of Nature. Thus they reached perfection, approving only those things which, if challenged, can be explained on grounds of the truth.'

Footnote: '——*and Use, &c.*': Dalton is referring to George Berkeley (1685–1753)'s philosophical dialogue *Alciphron: Or, The Minute Philosopher in Seven Dialogues*, 3rd edn (London J. & R. Tonson and S. Draper, 1752), pp. 120–27, wherein the interlocutors Alciphon and Euphranor discuss the relation of beauty to notions of proportion, symmetry, harmony, and order.

Appendices

APPENDIX I

James Eyre Week's *Poetical Prospects of Workington and Whitehaven* (1752)

James Eyre Weeks (c.1720–1775?) was born in Cork, and he appears to have studied at Trinity College, Dublin, c.1735–1739.[1] Week's *Poetical Prospect of Workington* was published in Whitehaven in 1752, and it was reprinted with his *A Poetical Prospect of Whitehaven* in the same year. The text presented below has been reproduced from this latter printing using the copy held in the Jackson Library, Carlisle City Library, Carlisle (J134).

A
POETICAL PROSPECT
OF
The COAST TOWN and HARBOUR
OF
WORKINGTON.
To which is Annexed a CORRECT EDITION
OF
The POETICAL PROSPECT
OF
WHITEHAVEN,

Both Written in the YEAR MDCCLII.

By JAMES EYRE WEEKS.
Formerly of TRINITY COLLEGE, DUBLIN.

Portus bene tutæ Carinis. [2]
VIRGIL.

JMartin.

WHITEHAVEN:
Printed for the AUTHOR, in the YEAR 1752.

A Poetical Prospect of Workington.

When surly March call'd forth his Russian Blasts,
When the bleak Tempest all the deep o'ercasts,
When the Ram's Fleece with solar influence burns,
Just as the Vernal Æquinox returns,
High swell'd the ocean with o'erteeming tides,
Which whiten foaming on the Coast-bank sides.

The Gull, sagacious of the brooding Storm,
Quits Shore, and up the Land seeks Shelter warm,
The Tenants of the Fields close refuge take
Near the thick hedge, fell Winds the Forest shake,   10
Chief on the Coast the menace of the Main,
Hangs imminent, with sweeping Clouds and Rain,
Now bursts the terror, black'ning all the Shore,
Down the Contents accumulated pour,
Forth rushes the fork'd lightnings sulphurous Flame
And all abroad the blue-ey'd Flashes stream.

   Now grouls the Thunder on the astonish'd Ear
While sighing owners for their Vessels fear,
All is dismay — the driving Squalls more fierce,
Burst on the Surge and o'er the Billows pierce,   20
When lo! at distance, struggling with the Blast
Appears the long contending shatter'd Mast,
Her TOPMAST gone——now nearer to the View;
Her Men appear——a disconcerted Crew!

   On her *beam-ends* she lies, all prone to sink,
Her op'ning *bows*, the watry ruin drink;

Under her *bare-poles*[3] now her *Yards*[4] confess,
Without a *skreed*[5] sail of her *Crank*[6] distress,
While ev'n the Helm, as conscious of its fear,
Neglects its wonted task the Ship to steer;   30
All pump for life, the Seaman in amaze,
Looks round agast for life——and fervent prays,
To him who rules the Terrors of the deep,
Who dictates to the Waves what bound to keep,
When lo!——perhaps the effect of earnest Pray'r,
The Storm subsides, the tempest threatens fair,
And WORKINGTON'S safe Harbour now receives,
The righted Vessel from the restless Waves.

   Ev'n Joys surprize is oftentimes too great!
And sinks, like Grief with overpow'ring weight;   40

   Behold a fainting Virgin borne ashore,
Who only with despair was fix'd before:
The blood and Spirits which around her Heart,
Had crouded first, now languishing depart,
And having Life and safety in her Eye,
She swoons with Joy to see deliverance nigh.

   Suspended thus betwixt his Life and Death,
The Soldier sentenced, panting heaves for breath,
But a Reprive, if he with transport hear,
And unexpected Life, salutes his Ear,   50
If, as the Muskets levell'd at his Breast;
Present to fire, his Pardon is exprest,
The Flood the Torrent of his joy runs high,
And drowns his Sense in rushing Agony.

From the Mines to the Mountains

    The Sun, who while the Storm was fierce and loud
Had taken shelter Safe behind a Cloud,
Now ventur'd forth——his sudden beam display'd,
The blythest prospect from the gloomiest Shade,
My sympathising Heart, which in my Breast
Had heav'd and flutter'd for the Crew distrest,   60
Now shar'd their Joys, and viewing them ashore,
My fears were hush'd and with the Tempest o'er.

    The heaving Ocean rock'd it's self [sic] to sleep,
Smooth'd were the wrinkl'd Furrows of the deep,
The finny Natives of the placid Sea,
Bask in the Calm-shine, and enjoy the Ray;
Now Lights returning beam creates anew,
And calls to Life the animated View.

    So when the Chaos indigested lay,
And darkness reign'd Primeval to the Day,   70
Th' Almighty Fiat sounded thro' the void,
And Space immense the broad Ey'd Beam enjoy'd,
Nature the plastic[7] Ward obedient heard,
And lo the burnish'd Universe appear'd,
The Gay-rob'd World forth issu'd to the Eye
Clad like a Bride in finish'd drapery:

    Where down the Mountains, thro' the extended Plain,
The *Derwent* pours his Tribute to the Main,
The *Derwent*, from the title fam'd, of one
Whose flight misguided soar'd too near a Throne,   80
Thro' a long rugged[8] Chain of hills he flows;
Near *Skiddow's* heighth, still white with Winter Snows[.]

Fast by his Foot a Friendly Port appears,
The hope and Anchor of the Seaman's fears.
Northwest the farthest on the English Coast,
Whose Harbour, Art-assisted, were its boast
Thine WORKINGTON the Land-lock'd Ship shall find
Thy Shore a refuge from the Seas and Wind,
Near thee, no Pangs the Mariner shall feel;
Thy friendly Sands still faithful to his Keel,   90
For shelter'd here by hills, on ev'ry side;
The Ships in safety, and undamag'd ride.

In Situation if we next survey,
How aptly plac'd to build a beauteous Quay,
In its dry bottom suited to receive
In dock, the Vessel shatter'd by the Wave:

How well might Wealth a general good bestow,
Ill-spent alas! In luxury and Shew,
Riches but in their *Use* conspicuous shine,
A barren glitter in the Chests confine.   100

See what our Ancestors for us have done!
How plann'd, how toil'd, thro' each revolving Sun!
What cost expended and what Thought bestow'd?
To sweeten Life upon the imbitter'd Road!

See the inclemency's of Earth and Sky,
From Man averted by Man's Industry,
See Forests fell'd, no more extend their shade;
But let in purer Æther thro' the Glade,
Lo! ev'ry Element subdu'd to Use,
See the drain'd Fen a wholesome Crop produce;   110

From the Mines to the Mountains

    See Cities built, where Ocean's roll'd before;
And Piers oppos'd against the Tempests pow'r,
See Trade her Vehicles thro' boistrous Seas;
Roll dauntless, for our luxury or Ease;
Lo! the ripe Produce of the Foreign Mart!
And Shores remote, connected by her Art!
Behold our Wealth superfluous wasted o'er;
To distant Climes, a rich, and valu'd Store,

    See *Public* Spirit, like a *Leaven*, breathe;
Thro' Nature's *dough* around, above, beneath!   120
And shall Posterity inactive Sleep!
Nor give its Sons as rich a Crop to reap?
Let not the Sire be blemish'd in the Son,
But expedite the Work so well begun;
Lo! ev'n a Century's increase has made,
From the mean fishing Boat, the Ship of Trade,
And where the Village hut was seen before,
A peopl'd Town now dignifies the Shore!

    From *Chapel-Hill*, whose ample View Surveys
A Tract extensive, both of Land and Seas;   130
Hoary *St. Bee* his awful summit rears,
Whose southern point the farthest Land appears,
Northward to *Ellenfoot*[9] the view extends,
And in a jutting Promontory Ends,

    On Galloway's hills amid unev'n heights
See Crophel's snowy head the Eye Delights.

    North East to *Anan* winds the Scottish Coast,
Where in a point the length'ning Channels lost;

Weeks: *Workington*

Near to *Carlisle* the Navigation tends
At *Rowcliff*, where the River Eden ends.   140
All along the Shore are little Creeks and Bays;
Which shelter Vessels from th' invading Seas,
Holme, *Alanby* and *Bownesse*;[10] shelter Form:
Where Ships draw up against th' approaching Storm,

    The smaller Craft here make their quick return,
And for their freight take in the Country Corn;
For well inhabited the Villas rise,
And plenteous tillage meets the roving Eyes!
In *Hundy*, *Skoose*, and *Seaton*[11] there you see;
The Cartage plying from the Colliery,   150
The *Land-banks*[12] there with jetty Treasures teem;
Fertile, and ripen'd by the Solar beam,
Where'er you look, on ev'ry side around;
The Coal-mines num'rous in the hills abound;

    There down the Pits descend the human moles,
And pick the Passage thro' the Veiny Coals,
Maintain thro' ev'ry obstacle their Way,
And force their entrance ev'n beneath the Sea,
All as their dangr'ous Conquests they Extend,
The Works with mighty Pillars they defend,   160
To prop the pondrous Roof that hangs above,
Which threatens Ravage to their deep Alcove;

    Tremendous crush! How dreadfully they die,
Then ill supported, tumbling from on high,
Upon their heads the heavy Ruins lye

    So mightier Shock! at St. DOMINGO'S ISLE[13]

From the Mines to the Mountains

The Earth's fierce Ague threatn'd many a Mile,
Till op'ning wide, the gaping Chasm displays,
The Steep down horrid Gulph, whose quick embrace,
Shuts in the num'rous Villages around,   170
While Shrieks of thousands echo under ground,
All, sudden bury'd, quick, beneath the deep,
Taken in Business, Pleasure, or in Sleep.

    Adventerous Man! How restless is thy Skill!
Thy search how Studious, how perverse thy will,
What can the mazes of thy wit escape?
What shun the changes of thy Proteus[14] shape?
Now high in Counsel with the stars of night,
Anon beneath in Caverns, hid from light,
Now on th' excentric Comet shot away   180
To space remote, amid the blaze of day,
And now pent up within a Cell, recluse,
Poring on Emmets, or on things abstruse,
Now in the Ken of Algebraic thought,
Then groveling low upon the Number 0.

    For thee cou'd Sleeping[15] Thunders latent lye
Or tawny Mines escape thy curious Eye[16]
The Steel, a stranger to the Flint's pent fire,
Know nothing, till you taught it to enquire,
The lurking Di'mond, hid in shades of night,   190
Know not it's [sic] Price, till valu'd by thy Sight,
Not ev'n Earth's *fuel*, meant to keep her warm,
Escape the savage of thy lawless Storm,
She bleeds deep wounded thro' her inmost Veins,
And yields her treasures with a Mother's Pains.
    For Ellenfoot and Camarton and Skoose,

Clifton and Harrington the Mine produce,
The[16] Villages thick Planted near the Sea,

A Rural Prospect from the Shore display,
There Seaton, Stainborn, Flimby, Dearham shew, 200
A Scene of Plenty near a Waste of Snow,
While on each Hand appears a vary'd Scene,
A Chaos luring on an Eden's Plain;

    The beauteous[18] Villas and the spreading Woods
Contrast the barren hills and distant Floods,
The ELLEN and the *Derwent's* peaceful Maze,
Strength'n the bleaker Prospect of the Seas;
True to the Wind, or sometimes prone to Veer
The Vanes of Shipping sporting high in Air,
As WORKINGTON and ELLENFOOT appear. 210

    There from the Ocean[19] Engines lift the Wave,
Destin'd again in briny Foam to rave,
By powerful heat behold the Snowy Sea,
In fuming rage Evaporate away,
While Nature's petrifying fetters bind,
The Salts and leave the Silver wealth behind.

    O'er Views Romantic while my Fancy roves,
Near old remains, which Contemplation loves,
Mid ancient Forts, with awful Ivy Crown'd,
Or Groves where *Druids* trac'd the hallow'd Ground, 220
Thus spoke the hoary Genius of the Place,
Tho' barren Wreaths thy greener temples grace.

    Yet oh! in time, suspend the trifling Song,

From the Mines to the Mountains

Nor to regardless Years the theme prolong,
For few alas! the muses now have Charms,
Turn turn thy thoughts to action, Trade, or arms,
Too delicate for Iron souls thy Strains,
By Nymphs unnoted, and unheard by Swains,
Proul with the Lion, and the Man of Prey,
Range the wild Desart, beat the trackless Sea,   230
But never hope thy Lot to mend or raise,
By Dreams of fancy, or by barren Lays,
Think not thy Fortune or to raise, or mend,
By envy'd Arts, which ne'er create a Friend.

    South from the Hill, *Whitehaven's* brows appear,
And West the eye takes in the point of Aire,
Kirkudbright's Ross north-east salutes the sight
And *Lamplough* Hills display their eastern height,
Near against *Seaton, Stainborn's* Village stands
And from it's [sic] brow a rural view commands.   240

    There on a Rock magnificently high
Stands *Curwen's* Hall, and with superiour Eye
Sees the proud Derwent swiftly rolling by,
Hence opening Vistas, and extended Vales,
A vary'd groupe of shaggy Woods and Dales,
A view compos'd of Hill, Coast, Town, and Main,
Of sylvan Forest, and of stretching Plain,
The vocal Bush, the Germinating trees,
The winding River Perfum'd by the Breeze;
From spreading Gardens to the Sense diffus'd,   250
With Nature's mingl'd elegance amus'd;

    Now lives the River with the Salmon's Fry,

Now leaps the Trout to catch th' insidious fly,
The Nets are cast to Catch the num'rous Brood,
Of the young Salmon ripning [sic] in the flood,
Above the Coops with a Weyre restrain,
The sporting Fish from rushing to the Main,
While o'er the Banks, with quiv'ring rod in Hand,
To catch the Prey, behold the Angler stand.

    Around a Scene of Rural Views arise,   260
The Plenteous Village there salutes the Eyes
Beneath the harmless flocks are seen to feed!
And Ploughs prepare the fallow for the Seed,
Now yean the Lambs,[20] now frisking sport their young,
Wag the glad Tail, and range the Walks along?
The Rabbits burrough all along the Shore;
And calmly sport tho' frequent Tempests roar;

    Thus in the Robe of Innocence array'd,
The peaceful Shepherd haunts the Rural Shade,
A Foe to Party or ambitious Guile;   270
He sees calm plenty round the Cottage smile,
To all the Terrors of the War unknown;
The Pomp of State, or tumult of a Throne.

            FINIS.

A Poetical Prospect of Whitehaven.

In that calm season when the mind is clear
From ev'ry bias, or of guilt or fear,
When the soul's vacant for impressions new,
Like the fair canvas for the limner's hue,
As such a time, for rising hills, my sight
Took in from PROSPECT, a refin'd delight,
From PROSPECT, gayest pleasure of the eye,
Ravish'd with nature's rich variety.

    From mist, or vapour was the Æther free,
And the air's temper did with mine agree,   10
Reflected on the deep Cerulean plain,
Bright Phoebus[21] seem'd the neptune[22] of the main;
Fair to the view was ev'ry object seen
'Twixt the green ocean, and the blue serene,
Whose billows seem'd the vaulted roof to lave,
While the horizon stoop'd to drink the wave.

    Above the eternal pencil had pourtray'd,
The soft and stronger touch of light and shade,
Diffus'd thro' regions of unbounded space,
The due proprieties of time and place;   20
Fix'd to their spheres the less and greater light,
And strew'd the concave with the seeds of night.

    Oh can there be, said I, a wretch so mean
To tax the Painter, yet behold the scene?
Who deals his gifts, in such proportion round,
That all is beauty, all is order found!

Where fair WHITEHAVEN opens to the west
Her friendly port, to give the seaman rest,
From tow'ring hills, whose brows the harbour form,
And promise shelter from the madding storm,   30
Far rov'd my eye —— on Caledonia's shore
The surge incessant beat with distant roar,
While Scotia's heights with pride behold the wave
Foam at their feet, and impotently rave:

   The neighb'ring ISLE, which boasts a peculiar sway,
Bore on the left, beneath the western ray;
The town of WORKINGTON, whose beacon lightning
Directs the seaman, lay upon my right,
Her vessels like a distant forest, shew
And seem upon the Ocean's verge to grow.   40
There Sancta Bega's sacred point extends
And o'er the billows venerably bends.

   Before my view an ample bason pours
Her waves swift rolling on to western shores.
While num'rous masts beneath, delight the eye,
The growth, WHITEHAVEN, of thy Industry,
There infant Parton's neighb'ring village hails
Her mother town, and spreads her lesser sails.
So, when a ship from western India rides
And richly frighted loads th' embracing tides,   50
Her buoy at distance chears the merchant's eyes,
And points to shew him where the Anchor lies:

   Nor thou, WHITEHAVEN, grudge thy parent shade
For Scarce a century can boast thy trade,
Nor four score suns have run their courses o'er,

From the Mines to the Mountains

Since a few fishing huts adorn'd thy shore.
Behold the pow'r of trade and Industry!
A mighty hive appearing from a Bee![23]
Thus great attempts from low beginnings rise
And what once weakly craul'd, now braves the skies.   60

   Near are the coalworks, LOWTHER'S treasur'd mines,
Whence the foul-air, thro' artful tube refines,
Like a Volcano the perennial Flame
Sulphureous burns in nature much the same,
Yet so by art contriv'd that thro' the fire,
The pestilential vapour may transpire,
The air expurg'd above, and free to breathe,
Th'adventrous collier works insur'd beneath.

   Think you, who (plac'd before th' enliv'ning heat
Furnish'd by him) your dainty viands eat,   70
For a short moment think upon the woe,
That he sustains, who restless toils below,
Debarr'd the light of heav'n, the Æther pure,
Think what the hardy collier must endure!
Who eats his scanty meal, in exile pent,
To give you warmth, and furnish you Content,
Or, when your frost nipp'd fingers seek the fire,
To his deep cavern let your thoughts retire,
There paint a Mortal, who has barter'd ease,
The sun's gay lamp, and noon's refreshing breeze,   80
Black as a fiend, who toils imprison'd there,
Nor joys, what even meanest wretches share,
The all reviving sun, and common air,
Then pour to heaven the meek, the grateful thought,
That plac'd your fortunes in a milder lot.

Great are thy pow'rs, oh! art, which can reform
The rage of whirlwinds, and controul the storm,
Can turn the rage of floods, direct their course,
And point them channels, where to spend their force
Which with the elements can war engage,   90
And shew the flames fell fury where to rage!

　　　Lo! here a lifeless waggon at thy will,
True to its ambit, circles round a hill,
Down the descent by Spedding's wond'rous art,
The waggon-way retains the flying cart.
So far from being cumber'd with its freight,
Like virtue———see it grows beneath a weight,
Down plains inclin'd the self-mov'd engines fly
To load the Ships which near the Hurry's lie.
Thro' wooden spouts descends the sooty ore,   100
An export grateful to HIBERNIAS[24] [sic] shore.

　　　So thro' the porous strata of the earth
Pervades the Ocean, giving springs a birth,
Then down the mountain's side they force away,
Pour o'er the plains and rush again to sea.

　　　Behold the mariners their talks pursue!
Lo! artists bent on bus'ness ever new,
Business for ever doing, never done,
Setting with night, and rising with the sun!
Business, like virtue, is its own reward,   110
Hence flows the goblet at the plenteous board,
While sloth with folded hands in anguish pines,
Or begs for scraps, or on an offal dines:

From the Mines to the Mountains

    See sweating Cyclops o'er the Anchor toil,
In proper time th' elastick blows recoil.
There from the ductile hemp the threads are spun,
Which into complicated cordage run,
Hence the best bow'r his solid structure takes
Nor (tho' the floods and tempests strain him breaks,
Emblem of union! Where collective force,   120
(Not feeble parties) stem oppressions course.

    While some the damage of the deep repair,
Others the virgin launch for sea prepare,
Conscious of maiden innocence she steers
Thro' untry'd dangers, and a world of fears,
Wedded, for foreign wealth to am'rous tides,
She shrinks as soon as Ocean clasps her sides,
Then dauntless spanks it thro' the briny main,
And sells her virgin innocence for gain,
Haply for many a voyage comes to port,   130
While yet her sails the flatt'ring breezes court,
While yet each thriving voyage is her boast,
Fraught with the riches of the golden coast,
At length like other beauty's she decays,
Her crazy side the faithless leak betrays,
On the false rock amid the dreary waste
(Ah! what avails her golden freight! she's cast.)

    To SOLWAY'S Firth extends the length'ning Bay,
Where ocean's life in sholes luxuriant play,
The royal Herring here supports his reign,   140
Source of our strength, as treasure on the main,
Her infant Buss, WHITEHAVEN too prepares,
And in her net the golden prey insnares;

Large and abundant too, the Oyster boasts
Peculiar sweetness on her winding coasts,
While to receive the life-restoring tide,
Her pearl-enamell'd folding-gates divide.

    Involv'd in smoke beneath the view, appear
A maze of streets,———lo busy commerce there
Hums frequent, in their various garb display'd,   150
Up from the Carter to the Lord of Trade,
While there the gardens prominent display
Their southern wall-fruits to the rip'ning ray.

    Here a retreat for ships, a port secure
Lands the rich import at the merchant's door,
The perfum'd leaf VIRGINIA'S rich produce
In our dense Air of medicinal use,
The golden leaf from western regions brought Down,
Thro' ev'ry branch of manufacture wrought;
Holds here unrivall'd its extensive mart,   160
And shifts thro' ev'ry mode of varying Art.

    Thy leaf, Tobacco, long has flourish'd here,
Pleasant concomitant of potent beer,
Sweet clouds of incense grateful to the skies,
In perfum'd odours at thy altars rise.

    Thro' infinite canals see traffick run!
While the fair stranger's hail'd by ev'ry sun!
Some hew th' extended tree, a future mast,
Destin'd to stand the north's tempestuous blast,
How far securer was its Forest-state!   170
How happier far its sequester'd retreat!

From the Mines to the Mountains

While yet by no ambitious views betray'd,
It's leafy honours form'd the hermit's shade,
O'er less extent, what tho' it reign'd obscure,
Yet in retirement was its reign secure,
Whilst in its boughs the songsters of the sky,
Form'd their gay orchester of melody,
Now doom'd alas to visit distant lands,
Or fall perhaps the wreck of faithless sands!

Till commerce was, how dark th' unletter'd mind,   180
Unconscious of the General———Mankind!
Mean was its province, circumscrib'd its sphere,
Nor knew beyond the winding coast to steer.
Each gale then drove the vessel back to shore,
Fearful the farther ocean to explore,
Nor knew the changes of another Zone,
Nor knew another sun besides their own.

Hail traffick! Ever honour'd———Vast thy use!
Hence fleets the growth of ev'ry clime produce,
Hence what revenues to the Crown accrue!   190
And hence protection to the subject too.

What constituted BRITAIN o'er the main
The sovereign mistress—dread of France and Spain?
But mighty commerce—from the merchant mann'd,
Her fleets shake terror o'er each hostile land,
From thee bright commerce, beauty too enjoys
Her richest dress,———and ev'n her darling toys:

Nor here let fav'rite beauty want a line,
Where with the graces, Virtue's charms combine,

Let not WHITEHAVEN'S daughters fair, as chaste,   200
Nor less in form excelling, than in taste,
Complain we paid not the respectful lay,
Cold were a PROSPECT, shut from Beauty's ray,
Beauty shall throw a lustre on the line,
Strengthen our view, and make the PROSPECT shine,
Their charms we honour, but their virtues more,
The amiable we love———the chaste adore.

  Here o'er thy brows WHITEHAVEN let me rove,
And see the secret springs of commerce move
Beneath, what subterraneans toil around!   210
Below, above, what curious arts abound!
Damag'd Tobaccos thro' a pipe transpire,
Nor taint the town with their offensive fire;
Here Salt, there Copperas various hands employs,
And smiling trade her golden reign enjoys.

  Oh Commerce honour'd by the wise and great!
Thou sure, and strongest cement of a state!
Ev'n liberty to thee her blessings owes,
Her peace at home, as conquest o'er her foes,
Wisdom thro' thee the vary'd moral sees,   220
From the false Æthiop, to the sly Chinese,[25]
The growth of ev'ry region round surveys,
Or hears her Maker worship'd several ways,
Makes an abridgement in her mind, of MAN,
From her own EUROPE to remote JAPAN.

FINIS.

Notes to Appendix One

1 See, Patrick Fagan, *A Georgian Celebration: Irish Poets of the Eighteenth Century* (Dublin: Branar, 1989), pp. 120–23.
2 '*A safe harbour for watchful ships*'; Weeks's epigraph would appear to be an adaptation on Virgil *Aeneid* (II.23): 'statio male fida carinis' (an unsafe harbour for ships).
3 *Bare-poles*: masts; see 'bare, adj., adv., and n.', *Oxford English Dictionary* <http://www.oed.com> (accessed 5 June 2018).
4 *Yards*: the spars on a mast which support the sails; see 'yard, n.2', *Oxford English Dictionary* <http://www.oed.com> (accessed 5 June 2018).
5 *Screed*: torn; see 'screed, n.1', *Oxford English Dictionary* <http://www.oed.com> (accessed 5 June 2018).
6 *Crank*: 'Liable to lean over or capsize; see 'crank, adj.2', *Oxford English Dictionary* <http://www.oed.com> (accessed 5 June 2018).
7 *Plastic*: 'easily moulded or shaped': see 'plastic, n. and adj.', *Oxford English Dictionary* <http://www.oed.com> (accessed 5 June 2018).
8 *Rugged*: 'having a broken, rocky, or uneven surface': see 'rugged, adj.1 and adv.', *Oxford English Dictionary* <http://www.oed.com> (accessed 5 June 2018).
9 Maryport.
10 Holme Cultram, Allonby, and Bowness-on-Solway.
11 Hunday, Scoose Farm, and Seaton.
12 The copy of Week's poem in the Jackson Library (J134) has a marginal annotation in black ink at the foot of the page that reads 'Coal-banks'.
13 Weeks is presumably referring to the Port-au-Prince earthquake of 1751.
14 Proteus: variable. The Greco-Roman sea god, Proteus, was capable of transforming himself into various shapes.
15 Gunpowder [Weeks's note].
16 Alluding to Coal mines [Weeks's note].
17 Kirkby, Ellerby, Dearham, Crosby, Allanby, Holme, Bowness, Rowcliffe, &c [Weeks's note].
18 Flimby Hall and Parks, Nether-hall, Unrigg hall [Weeks's note].
19 The Saltworks near Flimby [Weeks's note].
20 Literally, 'now lambs are born': see 'yean, v.', *Oxford English Dictionary*

<http://www.oed.com> (accessed 5 June 2018).
21 The sun: Phoebus is another name for Apollo, the Greco-Roman god of the sun.
22 A reference to the Roman god of the sea, counterpart of the Ancient Greek god Poseidon. The sense of the line is that the sun seemed lord of the sea.
23 At the return of Ships belonging to Whitehaven, at the Spanish invasion, was the BEE of ten Tons, and two Men, the largest on this Coast [Weeks's note].
24 Hibernia is the Latin name for Ireland.
25 Æthiop: Ethiopian. Such racist slurs were an unfortunate commonplace of eighteenth-century society.

APPENDIX II

Thomas Cowper's
A Poetical Prospect of Keswick (1752)

Thomas Cowper was the incumbent at Loweswater, in Cumberland, from 1744 until his death in 1795. His 'Poetical Prospect' of Keswick was written, so later reprintings of the work affirm, in 1752 and first published in 1775. The poem was re-printed at Cockermouth in 1851 (by T. Bailey and Son) and in 1863 (by E. Thwaites); it was also reprinted at Whitehaven in 1875 (by Callander and Dixon). Other, as yet unidentified, printings may exist. The editors have been unable to locate a copy of the 1775 edition of the poem. The text presented below has been reproduced from earliest of the known Victorian editions using the copy held in the Jackson Library, Carlisle City Library, Carlisle (J343).

A POETICAL

PROSPECT OF KESWICK

AND

THE PARTS ADJACENT,

WRITTEN IN THE SPRING OF THE YEAR 1752.

Nunc formosissimus Annus. VIRGIL.[1]

BY LATE T. COWPER,

Curate of Loweswater.

PRINTED ORIGINALLY IN THE YEAR
1775.

RE-PRINTED AT COCKERMOUTH BY T. BAILEY AND SON.
1851.

PRICE ONE PENNY.

From the Mines to the Mountains

A Poetical Prospect

In that calm season of the blooming year,
When trees and meadows in their pride appear;
Invited by the morning, cool and fair,
I walk'd the fields to taste the vernal air:
The storms were hush'd; in peace their fury laid,
And pearly dews hung twinkling on the glade,
Whilst o'er mankind sleep held his easy reign,
And beasts and birds in silence did remain,
All but the wakeful Lark, whose tuneful lay
Did from the sky salute the day.   10
A soft monition to the human race
With joyful lips to sing their Maker's praise.

    Thus, list'ning to the Lark's melodious song,
Thro' many a verdant field I post along,
Until at last I came where SKIDDAW shrouds
His hoary temples in a veil of clouds,
And TEN'RIFFE like, a faithful land-mark stands;
Seen by far distant seas and distant lands.
When thus advanc'd upon the rising ground,
Pleas'd I beheld the charming landscape round.   20

    Just so, methought, did ISRAEL's shepherd stand
On PISGAH's top,[2] and view'd the Promis'd Land:
He saw and wish'd; but could obtain no more
Than one bare prospect of that happy shore.

    Now first of all I view'd, distinct in sight,
The lake of BASSENTHWAITE upon my right;

Cowper: *Keswick*

Whose billows, glimm'ring with the Western ray.
Each evening add new lustre to the day.

    Thus candles burnt to socket blaze more high,
Take their last leave, and in an instant die.   30
See M<small>ILBECK</small>, A<small>PPLETHWAITE</small>, and L<small>YSSCK</small> too;
All shelter'd from the cold, by S<small>KIDDAW</small>'S brow.
At O<small>RMATHWAITE</small>, see B<small>ROWNRIGG</small>'S ancient seat,
Rudely majestic, and obscurely great;
But which, in fame and splendour, soon will rise,
Ennobled by a Doctor[3] learned and wise.
At some small distance, see where Vic'rage stands,
And charming prospects ev'ry way commands;
Where handsome buildings, walks, and gardens neat,
Delight your eye, and form a fine retreat.   40
Almost adjoining, see the sacred[4] dome
To which the just t'adore their Maker come;
Where deep-ton'd bells, and relics of the dead,
Inspire the soul with reverential dread.

M<small>ONK</small> H<small>ALL</small> and C<small>ROSTHWAITE</small>, likewise fair H<small>IGH</small> H<small>ILL</small>,
Of old renown'd, see, where they flourish still.
Beyond the bridge, lo, K<small>ESWICK</small> doth appear,
Where's weekly sold, meal, butter, beer, and beer:[5]
In manufacture is its boasted trade;
Here wool is spun, and stuffs and serges made: 50
Here too great Stephenson[6] was born; a name

Rising illustrious in the lists of fame;
Whose splendid seat, and costly builds grace,
And long will be an honour to that place.
Hard by this town late grew a lofty[7] wood,

From the Mines to the Mountains

Upon the verge of DERWENT'S rolling flood.
Myriads of songsters perch'd amongst the trees,
And fill'd the place with sweetest harmonies.
Long found the cattle here a safe retreat
From winter's tempest, and from summer's heat: 60
But not without concern I now perceiv'd
Its doom was past, too far to be repriev'd.
That ancient wood, where beasts did safely rest,
And where the Crow long time had built her nest;
Now falls a destin'd prey to savage hands,
Being doom'd, alas! to visit distant lands.
Ah! what avails thy boasted strength at last?
That brav'd the rage of many a furious blast;
When now thy body, spent with many a wound,
Loud groans its last, and thunders to the ground;   70
Whilst hills, and dales, and woods, and rocks resound.

   Here DERWENT, like a miser, not content
With narrow limits, spreads to vast extent;
Where boats and islands make a pleasing sight,
And yield at once both profit and delight.
Here waves a harvest,[8] there a noble wood,[9]
And yonder oxen[10] graze all in the flood.

   See where the Great for pleasure stem the tide,
And o'er the waves on wooden horses[11] ride.
Lo there a jaded palfrey[12] homeward steers,   80
All soak'd with nets, and shakes its dabbed ears.
One bears a load; another at tail[13]
Drags slowly on a most enormous trail.

   Thus boats and waves are taught to serve instead

Cowper: *Keswick*

Of horses and waggon, to supply your need,
Such numerous ways there are for industry
To save from want and dire necessity.

   Hence DERWENT, like MEANDER, winding flows,
From town to town; just as the carrier goes:
'Till come at last to WORKINGTON its coast,   90
It plunges in the seas, and there is lost.

   Next CASTLE RIGG appears, in stately show,
And views distinct the verdant plain below.

   Southward, at distance, see the winding vale
And rugged mountains of old BORROWDALE,
Whose *Black Lead Mine* is fam'd thro' many a coast;
Nor can whole EUROPE such another boast.
Here the first mountains past, new mountains rise,
And mountains still behind out-brave the skies.
Adown the rocks, hark how the torrent roars;   100
And noisy cascades fill the distant shores.

   Lo, NEWLANDS too in her green mantle shines;
Long since renowned for her *Copper Mines*.
HOWE, ULLOCK, THRONTHWAITE, and the BRAITHWAITES too,
With all their flow'ry orchards, stands to view.

   Before me lay a wide extended plain,
Well fraught with crops of herbage and of grain,
The trees and hedges, which adorn'd the scene,
Stood finely deck'd in beauteous living green:
See, how the meadows, vales, and pleasing bow'rs   110
Are all embroider'd with the finest flow'rs!

From the Mines to the Mountains

Like those bright spangles, which adorn the night,
And deck the concave with a glitt'ring light.
So great the pow'r of an Almighty hand,
To frame a world, or to adorn a land!
In vain the Painter pores, and daubs and spies;
His awkward piece th' original belies;
And boasted Art, when all her lengths she's run,
Must own herself by Nature far outdone.

   See how the bees, those more than chymists sure,   120
Extract the nectar from each od'rous flow'r:
And yet (the world may wonder for to see't),
Nor wound the substance, nor impair the sweet.
See, how, ev'n at the lot meridian hour,
They ply their work, and haste from flow'r to flow'r.
Go, mortals, then to the laborious bee,
And learn a lesson of true industry:
Learn what blest fruit on joint endeavours waits;
Union preserves both families and states.

   Just in the centre of the flow'ry green,   130
A river[14] flows both cool and crystalline;
Then finny tribes, as nature to them gave,
Lascivious wanton in the silver wave.
The cattle stand within the cooling stream,
Secure from thirst, and scorching PHOEBUS' beam.
The current laves the meadows, as it flows;
And yields rich plenty wheresoe'er it goes.
An emblem of a great and gen'rous mind,
That strives t' advance the good of all mankind.

   With transport next, I view the rising ear,   140

And all the product of th' advancing year;
Till'd by the painful and industrious hand,
The fields luxuriant with rich plenty stand;
While sloth's half till'd, half cultivated ground,
Does ev'ry where with thorns and weeds abound.

    Blest industry! what plenty crowns thy hand!
From thee what stores diffuses thro' the land!
See, what profusion yonder vallies bring!
See, how the fields with corn do laugh and sing!
Thrice happy they, said I, whose care and pains,   150
Are here rewarded with such ample gains.
They steal away their lives in quiet here,
Unsour'd by passion, uninslav'd with fear:
Here no ambitious views their souls molest;
No anxious cares disturb their easy rest.
Long live, ye swains; to heaven and earth right dear:
Secure of plenty, and a conscience clear!

    From fields of corn the beauteous prospect led
To verdant pastures where the cattle fed,
Where also view another pleasing scene,   160
Whole herds of oxen grazing on the green.
Some lay to rest; some hasten to the wood;
Whilst others cool their bodies in the flood.
The cows stand lowing in a nearer vale;
And wait, with dugs distended, for the pail:
A wholsome [sic] liquor ready to afford
Unto their grateful, may be thankless lord.

    Thus doth kind heav'n unnumber'd gifts bestow
On us ungrateful mortals here below;

From the Mines to the Mountains

    And does, without distinction, blessings shed   170
Both on the righteous and the sinful head.
Hence cheese and butter, plain but sweet repast!
Food not unworthy of a monarch's taste!
And fed by them the farmer turns the soil;
His hardy limbs are strong and fit for toil.

    Thus mortals liv'd in earlier ages born,
And eat, for food, milks, roots, and ears of corn;
Inur'd to toil, they at an hundred years,
Brought to their grave their mem'ry, eyes, and ears.

    At farther distance may your eye behold   180
Vast flocks of sheep, with many an ample fold;
See where the sportive lambs all frisk and bound,
And play delightful gambols all around.

    Thus thoughtless youth consume in wanton play
Th' unvalued treasures of many a glorious day;
Till age comes on, and death sweeps all away!

    Meantime the shepherd from some distant rock
With glee beholds his jolly thriving flock;
And when the Sun's in Cancer mounted high,
He drives them to a fold the river nigh;   190
And soon does wash them in the swelling flood;
And afterwards he shears the fleecy load.

    Thus having shorn his sheep, the shepherd swain
Feasts with his fellow-joggers of the plain.
And at such time, see, how his cleanly board
Is with all kinds of rural dainties stor'd,

Enough to please the palate of a lord.
And whilst they share, in peace, such wholesome meat,
They envy not the tables of the great.
When feasting's done the ample goblet's crown'd,   200
And with a toast goes merrily around:
Nor cease full bumpers, till the morning ray
Has chas'd both sorrows and the stars away.

   Next, when refreshed, see where the champion goes,
To well grown meadows where he stoutly mows.
See, how the grass, cut by his glitt'ring blade,
To hay soon withers, and is home convey'd.

   Just so the young, the vig'rous, and the brave,
Are snatch'd by death, and lodged in the grave!

   See, how with rakes, on ev'ry side they run;   210
And toil and sweat to get their labour done;
And make their hay before the setting sun.

   Reproof severe! to those who spend their time,
Of heav'n unmindful, and its joys sublime!
Who all life's sunshine, leave their work undone;
Nor mind repentance till their race is run!

   More neat the orchards I with pleasure view,
Like spotless vestals, clad in shining hue.
Here art and nature both together meet,
To make the prospect ev'ry way complete.   220
So where bright parts and education join,
They make the man bright as the sun to shine.
See, how the trees with fragrant blossoms swell,

From the Mines to the Mountains

Right pleasing to the sight, and sweet to smell.
But soon, ah! soon, the fragrance breathes its last;
The lustre fades; the transient blossoms waste!
The blooming amid, we by experience find,
Is for the useful matron soon resign'd.
Hence autumn loads with fruit the bended tree;
Or to the table sends her progeny.   230
Hence many a basket to the market goes;
And many a bowl with sparkling liquor flows.
O may no raging blasts be heard around,
To dash these fruits untimely to the ground!
But safe may they upon the tree remain,
Till ripe they court the hand of ev'ry swain;
Or gently drop at last upon the plain.

Last, I beheld the tow'ring mountains rise,
That like huge ATLAS, seem'd to prop the skies.
See, how on ev'ry side their ridges stand,   240
Like Nature's bulwarks, to protect the land.
These too are with the richest treasures stor'd,
And to mankind abundant wealth afford.
Some for materials in their quarries roam,
To shelter or erect their stately dome.
Whilst others dive more deep, and strict explore
Their hidden caverns for the shining ore;
Here the industrious poor employment find,
To save from want, and benefit mankind.
Hence, tho' the mountains Nature's wilds may seem, 250
Yet are they useful, and deserve esteem;
For ev'n the wildest, meanest, craggy hill
Finds work for human industry and skill.

Thus having view'd the beauteous landscape's round,
And seen what diff'rence in its parts is found;
The Great Creator's skill I straight admire,
And soon my heart glows with religious fire.
Nor can I quit the scene, or end my lays,
Till I have tun'd my voice to chant his praise;
And let far distant hills and vallies ring,   260
Whilst thus I praise the Great Eternal King.

Notes to Appendix Two

1 'Now the year is at its fairest'; the quotation comes from Virgil's *Eclogues* (III.57).
2 Cowper is referring to Moses's vision of the Promised Land from the summit of Mount Pisgah in Deuteronomy 34:1–4.
3 Dr Brownrigg [Cowper's note].
4 Crosthwaite Church [Cowper's note].
5 Keswick received its market charter from King Edward I in 1276.
6 Edward Stephenson, Esq., Governor of Bengal [Cowper's note]. Stephenson (c.1691–1768) was born and died in Keswick.
7 The Crow Park, falling in the year 1752 [Cowper's note]. The oak grove at Crow Park began being removed as early as 1748. See Derek Denman, *Materialising Cultural Value*, pp. 89–97.
8 The Corn Island [Cowper's note].
9 The Lord's Island [Cowper's note].
10 St. Herbert's Isle [Cowper's note].
11 Pleasure Boats [Cowper's note].
12 A fishing Boat [Cowper's note].
13 Boats employed in bringing down Wood from Borrowdale [Cowper's note].
14 The River Derwent [Cowper's note].

BIBLIOGRAPHY

'An Abstract of the Poor Bills', *London Magazine*, 21 (April 1752), 153–54

A Catalogue of the Collection of Eighteenth-Century Printed Books and Manuscripts formed by Lord Rothschild, 2 vols (Cambridge: Privately printed at the University Press, 1954)

'*A Descriptive Poem, addressed to Two Ladies, at their return from viewing the mines near Whitehaven*', *Monthly Review*, 11 (December 1754), 487–89

'A List of Marriages for the Year 1750', *The Gentleman's Magazine*, 20 (February 1750), 91

A New and General Biographical Dictionary: Containing an Historical, Critical, and Impartial Account of the Lives and Writings of the Most Eminent Persons in Every Nation in the World, 12 vols (London: W. Strahan, 1795)

Addison, Joseph, *The Spectator*, 418 (30 June 1712), n. p.

Allen, J. S. 'The 1715 and other Newcomen Engines at Whitehaven, Cumberland', *Transactions of the Newcomen Society for the Study of the History of Engineering and Technology*, 44 (1975), 237–68

Amory, Thomas, *The Life of John Buncle, Esq; Containing Various Observations and Reflections, Made in several Parts of the World, and Many Extraordinary Relations*, 2 vols (London: J. Johnson and B. Davenport, 1766)

Barnard, John (ed.), *Alexander Pope: The Critical Heritage* (London: Routledge & Keegan Paul, 1973)

Beck, Rudolph, 'From Industrial Georgic to Industrial Sublime: English Poetry and the Early Stages of the Industrial Revolution', *British Journal for Eighteenth-Century Studies*, 27 (2004), 17–36

Beckett, J. V., 'Dr William Brownrigg, F.R.S.: Physician, Chemist and Country Gentleman', *Notes and Records of the Royal Society of London*, 31 (1977), 255–271

— — —, 'Lowther College 1697–1740: "For none but gentlemen's sons"', *Transactions of the Cumberland and Westmorland Antiquarian and Archaeological Society*, n.s. 79 (1979), 103–7

— — —, 'Illness and Amputation in the Eighteenth Century: The Case of Sir James Lowther', *Medical History*, 24 (1980), 88–92

— — —, J. V. Beckett, *Coal and Tobacco: The Lowthers and the Economic Development of West Cumberland, 1660–1760* (Cambridge: Cambridge University Press, 1981)

— — —, 'An Eighteenth-Century Case History: Carlisle Spedding 1738', *Medical History*, 26 (1982), 303–6

— — —, 'Carlisle Spedding (1695–1755), Engineer, Inventor and Architect', *Transactions of the Cumberland and Westmorland Antiquarian and Archaeological Society*, n.s. 83 (1983), 131–40

— — —, 'Inheritance and Fortune in the Eighteenth Century: The Rise of Sir James Lowther, Earl of Lonsdale', *Transactions of the Cumberland and Westmorland Antiquarian and Archaeological Association*, n.s. 87 (1987), 171–78

— — —, 'Lowther, Henry 3rd Viscount Lonsdale (1694–1751)', *Oxford Dictionary of National Biography*, 60 vols (Oxford: Oxford University Press, 2004), XXXIV, p. 636

— — —, 'Lowther, James, earl of Lonsdale (1736–1802)', *Oxford Dictionary of National Biography*, 60 vols (Oxford: Oxford University Press, 2004), XXXIV, pp. 625–28

— — —, 'Lowther, John, first Viscount Lonsdale (1655–1700),' *Oxford Dictionary of National Biography*, 60 vols (Oxford: Oxford University Press, 2004), XXXIV, pp. 634–36

Bending, Stephen, *Green Retreats: Women, Gardens and Eighteenth-Century Culture* (Cambridge: Cambridge University Press, 2013)

Berkeley, George, *Alciphron: Or, The Minute Philosopher in Seven Dialogues*, 3rd edn (London J. & R. Tonson and S. Draper, 1752)

Bicknell, Peter, *The Picturesque Scenery of the Lake District, 1752–1855: A Bibliography* (Winchester: St Paul's Bibliographies, 1990)

'Bill of Mortality from June 28 to July 26, 1763', *The Gentleman's*

Bibliography

Magazine, 33 (July 1763), 363

'Books publish'd in December; With Remarks', *The Gentleman's Magazine*, 24 (December 1754), 581

Brewer, John, *The Pleasures of the Imagination: English Culture in the Eighteenth Century* (New York: Farrar, Straus & Giroux, 1997)

Brown, John, *A Description of the Lake at Keswick* (Newcastle, 1767)

Bucholz, R. O. 'Semour, Charles, sixth duke of Somerset (1662–1748)', *Oxford Dictionary of National Biography*, 60 vols (Oxford: Oxford University Press, 2004), XLIX, pp. 857–60

Burke, Edmund, *Philosophical Enquiry into the Origins of Our Idea of the Beautiful and the Sublime* (London: R. and J. Dodsley, 1757)

Burkett, Mary E. and David Sloss (eds), *Read's Point of View: Paintings of the Cumbrian Countryside* (Kendal: Skiddaw Press, 1995)

Burn, Richard, *The History of the Poor Laws: With Observations* (London: A. Millar, 1764)

Burtchaell, G. D. and T. U. Sadleir (eds), *Alumni Dublinenses*, new edn (Dublin: Alexander Thomas & Co., Ltd., 1935)

Camden, William, *Britannia*, 5th edn (London: G. Bishop, 1600)

Claudian, *The Rape of Proserpine, from Claudian. In Three Books*, trans by Jabez Hughes (London: F. Burleigh, 1714)

Collier, Sylvia and Sarah Pearson (eds), *Whitehaven 1660–1800: A New Town of the Late Seventeenth Century* (London: HMSO, 1991)

Courtney, W. P. and John Wyatt, 'Dalton, John (1709–1763)', *Oxford Dictionary of National Biography*, 60 vols (Oxford: Oxford University Press, 2004), XIV, pp. 1013–14.

Cowper, Thomas, *A Poetical Prospect of Keswick, and the Parts Adjacent, Written in the Spring of the Year 1752* (Cockermouth: T. Bailey and Son, 1851)

Cranstone, David, *Whitehaven Coast Archeological Survey*, Bound Report for the National Trust (2006–2007) <http://www.lakestay.

co.uk/whitehavenmininghistory.html> (accessed 5 June 2018)

Cross, Richard, *The Metaphysics of the Incarnation: Thomas Aquinas to Duns Scotus* (Oxford: Oxford University Press, 2002)

Cumberland, Richard, *Odes* (London: J. Robson, 1776)

Dalton, John, *A Descriptive Poem, Addressed to Two Ladies, at their Return from Viewing the Mines near Whitehaven* (London: J. and J. Rivington, 1755)

– – –, 'A Descriptive Poem, Addressed to Two Ladies at Their Return from Viewing the Mines near Whitehaven', in George Pearch (ed.), *A Collection of Poems in Two Volumes, by Several Hands*, 2 vols (London: G. Pearch, 1768), I, pp. 23–43

– – –, *Two Epistles: The First, To a Young Nobleman from his Preceptor. Written in the year 1735-6. The second, To the Right Honourable the Countess of Hartford, At Percy Lodge: In the year 1744* (London: R. Dodsley, 1745)

Davidson, Edward H., 'Franklin and Brownrigg', *American Literature*, 23 (1951), 38–56

Defoe, Daniel, *A Tour thro' the Whole Island of Great Britain, Divided into Circuits or Journies*, 3 vols. (London: G. Strahan, 1727)

Denman, Derek, Materialising Cultural Value in the English Lake District: *A Study of the Responses of New Landowners to Representations of Place and People*, Unpublished PhD thesis (Lancaster University, 2011)

Desaguliers, John Theophilus, *Course of Experimental Philosophy*, Vol. 2 (London: W. Innys, et al., 1744)

'Discourses on several Subjects and Occasions. By John Dalton, D.D.', *The Critical Review, or, Annals of Literature*, 6 (August 1758), 121–25

Dixon, Joshua, *The Literary Life of William Brownrigg: To Which are Added An Account of the Mines Near Whitehaven* (London: Longman & Rees)

Donaldson, Christopher, Robert W. Dunning, and Angus J.L. Winchester (Eds), *Henry Hobhouse's Tour Through Cumbria in 1774* (Kendal: Cumberland and Westmorland Antiquarian and

Bibliography

Archaeological Society, 2018). Tract Series, no. 27

Emsley, Clive, Tim Hitchcock, and Robert Shoemaker, 'London History: London, 1715–1760', *Old Bailey Proceedings Online*, <www.oldbaileyonline.org> (accessed 5 June 2018)

Fagan, Patrick, *A Georgian Celebration: Irish Poets of the Eighteenth Century* (Dublin: Branar, 1989)

Fairer, David 'Georgic', in Jack Lynch (ed.), *The Oxford Handbook of British Poetry, 1660-1800* (Oxford: Oxford University Press, 2016), pp. 457–72

– – –, *Organising Poetry: The Coleridge Circle, 1790–1798* (Oxford: Oxford University Press, 2009)

Fiennes, Celia, *Through England on a Side Saddle in the Time of William and Mary* (London: Field and Tuer, 1888)

Foster, Joseph (ed.), *Alumni Oxonienses: The Members of the University of Oxford, 1500–1714*, 3 vols (Oxford: Parker & Co., 1891)

Founders Online, National Archives <https://founders.archives.gov/> (accessed 5 June 2018)

Gilpin, William, *Observations, Relative Chiefly to Picturesque Beauty, Made in the Year 1772*, 2 vols (London: R. Blamire, 1786)

Gray, J. M. (ed.), *Memoirs of the Life of John Clerk of Penicuik, Baronet* (Edinburgh: Scottish Historical Society, 1892)

Greteman, Blaine '"To Secure Our Freedom": How A Mask Presented at Ludlow-Castle Became Milton's Comus', in Blair Hoxby and Ann Baynes Coiro (eds), *Milton in the Long Restoration* (Oxford: Oxford University Press, 2016), pp. 143–58

Harris, John, *Lexicon Technicum: Or, An Universal English Dictionary of Arts and Sciences* (London: D. Brown, et al., 1704)

Haswell, J. F. (ed.), *The Registers of Lowther, 1540–1812* (Penrith: 'Herald' Publishing Co. Ltd., 1933)

Havens, R. D., *The Influence of Milton on English Poetry* (Cambridge, MA: Harvard University Press, 1922)

Hesiod, *Theogony and Works and Days*, ed. by M.L. West (Oxford:

Oxford University Press, 2000)
Hunter, Joseph (ed.), *The Diary of Ralph Thoresby, F.R.S.*, 2 vols (London: H. Colburn and R. Bentley, 1830)
Hutchinson, William, *The History of the County of Cumberland*, 2 vols (Carlisle: F. Jollie, 1794)
Hutchinson, William, *An Excursion to the Lakes in Westmorland and Cumberland; With a Tour through Part of the Northern Counties in the Years 1773 and 1774*, 2 vols (London: J. Wilkie, 1776)
Hutton, B. G., 'A Lakeland Journey, 1759', *Transactions of the Cumberland and Westmorland Antiquarian and Archaeological Society*, n.s., 61 (1961), 288–93
Hyde, Matthew, and Nikolaus Pevsner, *Cumbria: Cumberland, Westmorland and Furness* (New Haven and London: Yale University Press, 2010)
Jefferson, Samuel, *The History and Antiquities of Cumberland: With Biographical Notices and Memoirs*, 2 vols (Carlisle: F. Jefferson, 1842)
Johnson, Samuel, 'Life of Denham', *Prefaces, Biographical and Critical, to the Works of the English Poets*, 10 vols (London: J. Nichols, 1779–1781), IV, pp. 1–31
Jungnickel, Christa, and Russell K. McCormmach, *Cavendish* (Philadelphia, PA: The American Philosophical Society, 1996)
King, William, *Political and Literary Anecdotes of His Own Times* (London: J. Murray, 1818)
Lewis, W. S. (ed.), *The Yale Edition of Horace Walpole's Correspondence*, 48 vols (New Haven, CT: Yale, 1937–1983)
Lowther, James, 'An Account of the Damp Air in a Coal-Pit, Sunk within 20 Yards of the Sea', *Philosophical Transactions*, 429 (1753), 109–113
Magrath, John Richard (ed.), *The Flemings in Oxford: Being Documents Selected from the Rydal Papers in Illustration of the Lives and Ways of Oxford Men, 1650–1700*, 3 vols (Oxford: Clarendon Press, 1904–1924)
Mannex, P. J. (ed.), *History, Topography and Directory of*

Bibliography

Westmorland (London: Simpkin, Marshall & Co., 1849)

Masson, David, *The Life of John Milton: Narrated in Connexion with the Political, Ecclesiastical, and Literary History of His Time*, 6 vols (London: Macmillan & Co., 1859–1880)

Matthews, Stephen, *Beauty in the Lap of Horror: Early Travellers to Borrowdale and Derwentwater* (Carlisle: Bookcase, 2016)

– – –, *The Gentleman who Surveyed Cumberland: A description of Cumberland in the middle of the eighteenth century as found in the collected works of George Smith of Wigton and others* (Carlisle: Bookcase, 2014)

Metcalfe, R. W., *The Ravenstonedale Parish Registers*, 3 vols (Kendal: T. Wilson, 1893–1894)

Millward, Roy, and Adrian Robinson, *The Lake District* (London: Eyre and Spottiswoode, 1970)

Milton, John, *Complete Shorter Poems*, ed. by Stella P. Revard (Oxford: Wiley-Blackwell, 2009)

– – –, *Paradise Lost*, ed. by Alastair Fowler, 2nd edn (London: Routledge, 2013)

Morgan, Kenneth (ed.), *An American Quaker in the British Isles: The Travel Journals of Jabez Maud Fisher, 1775–1779* (Oxford: Oxford University Press, 1992)

Myers, Sylvia Harcstark *The Bluestocking Circle: Women, Friendship, and the Life of the Mind in Eighteenth-Century England* (Oxford: Oxford University Press, 1990),

Nicholson, I. S., and D.P. Sewell, 'History Notes on St. James's Church, Whitehaven', *Cumbria County History Trust* (2013), 37pp. <https://www.cumbriacountyhistory.org.uk/> (accessed 5 June 2018)

Nicholson, Norman *The Lakers: The Adventures of the First Tourists* (London: Robert Hale, 1955),

Nicolson, Joseph, and Richard Burn, *The History and Antiquities of the Counties of Westmorland and Cumberland*, 2 vols (London 1777)

Nightingale, B., *The Ejected of 1662 in Cumberland and Westmorland: Their Predecessors and Successors*, 2 vols

(Manchester: Manchester University Press, 1911)

O' Dwyer, Frederick, 'Robert West, Christopher Myers and St. James's Church, Whitehaven', *Journal of the Irish Georgian Society*, 12 (2010), 15–23

Owen, Hugh, *The Lowther Family: Eight Hundred Years of 'A Family of Ancient Gentry and Worship'* (Chichester: Phillimore & Co., 1990)

Pennant, Thomas, *A Tour in Scotland, and Voyage to the Hebrides, MDCCLXXII* (Chester: J. Monk, 1774)

Pennington, Montagu (ed.), *A Series of Letters Between Mrs. Elizabeth Carter and Miss Catherine Talbot*, 4 vols (1809)

Percy, Thomas (ed), *Reliques of Ancient English Poetry*, 2nd edn, 3 vols (London: J. Dodsley, 1767)

Pope, Alexander, *The Poems of Alexander Pope*, ed. by John Butt (New Haven, CT: Yale University Press, 1963)

Port, M. H., 'Lowther Hall and Castle', *Transactions of the Cumberland and Westmorland Antiquarian and Archaeological Association*, 81 (1981), 123–36

Powell, Cecilia and Stephen Hebron (eds), *Savage Grandeur and Noblest Thoughts: Discovering the Lake District, 1750–1820* (Grasmere: Wordsworth Trust, 2010)

Pratt, Herbert T., 'Brownrigg, William (1711–1800)', *Oxford Dictionary of National Biography*, 60 vols (Oxford: Oxford University Press, 2004), VIII, pp. 274–75

'Preferments', *The Royal Magazine* (August 1763), 112

Prevost, W. A. J., 'A Journie to Carlyle and Penrith in 1731', *Transactions of the Cumberland & Westmorland Antiquarian & Archaeological Society*, n.s. 61 (1961), 202–37

– – –, 'A Trip to Whitehaven to Visit the Coal-works There in 1739, By Sir John Clerk', *Transactions of the Cumberland & Westmorland Antiquarian & Archaeological Society*, n.s. 65 (1965), 305–19

Reynolds, Myra, *The Treatment of Nature in English Poetry Between Pope and Wordsworth* (Chiacgo: University of Chicago Press, 1896)

Bibliography

Roberts, William, *A Dawn of Imaginative Feeling: The Contribution of John Brown to Eighteenth Century Though and Literature* (Carlisle: Northern Scholar Press 1996)

Rollinson, William, *A History of Man in the Lake District* (London: J. M. Dent & Sons, 1967)

Sambrook, James, 'Seymour (née Thynne), Frances, duchess of Somerset (1699–1754)', *Oxford Dictionary of National Biography*, 60 vols (Oxford: Oxford University Press, 2004), XLIX, pp. 880–81

Shakespeare, William, *Titus Andronicus*, ed. by Jonathan Bate (London: Routledge, 1995)

Smith, George, 'Journey to the Black Lead Mines', *Gentleman's Magazine*, 21 (1751), 51–53

– – –, 'A Dreadful Storm in Cumberland', *Gentleman's Magazine*, 24 (1754), 464–65

Stainton, Lindsay, and Christopher White, *Drawing in England from Hilliard to Hogarth* (London: British Museum Publications, 1988)

Stukeley, William, *Itinerarium Curiosum; Or, An Account of the Antiquities and Remarkable Curiosities in Nature or Art Observed in Travels Through Great Britain*, 2 vols. (London: Baker & Leigh, 1776)

Sykes, John, *An Account of the Dreadful Explosion in Wallsend Colliery, on the 18th June, 1835* (Newcastle-upon-Tyne: J. Sykes, 1835)

Tickell, Thomas, *Oxford: A Poem* (London: E. Sanger, 1707)

Tierney, James E. (ed.), *The Correspondence of Robert Dodsley, 1733–1764* (Cambridge: Cambridge University Press, 1988)

Tyler, Ian, *Goldscope and the Mines of Derwent Fells* (Keswick: Blue Rock Publications, 2005)

Virgil, *The Aeneid*, trans. by Robert Fagles (London: Penguin Books, Ltd., 2006)

Virgil, *The Eclogues, The Georgics*, trans. by C. Day Lewis (Oxford: Oxford University Press, 1999)

Vitruvius, *The Ten Books on Architecture*, trans. by Morris Hicky

Morgan (Cambridge, MASS: Harvard University Press, 1914)

Walpole, Horace, *Memoires of the Last Ten Years of the Reign of George the Second*, 2 vols (London: J. Murray, 1822)

Ward, Jean E., 'The Sinking of Saltom Pit, Whitehaven', *Transactions of the Cumberland and Westmorland Antiquarian and Archaeological Society*, n.s. 91 (1991), 127–43

Warner, Richard, *A Tour through the Northern Counties of England*, 2 vols (Bath: R. Cruttwell, 1802)

Watson, William, 'An Account of a Treatise by Wm. Brownrigg M.D. F.R.S. intituled, "The Art of making common salt, as now practised in most parts of the world; with several improvements proposed in that art, for the use of the British dominions;" abstracted by W. Watson F.R.S.', *Philosophical Transactions*, 45 (1748), 351–72

Weeks, James Eyre, *A Poetical Prospect of the Coast Town and Harbour of Workington. To which is Annexed a Correct Edition of The Poetical Prospect Whitehaven* (Whitehaven: J. Weeks, 1752)

Wesley, John, *An Extract of the Reverend Mr. John Wesley's Journal, from July XX, 1750 to October 28, 1754* (London: J. Robinson and T. James, 1759)

Winchester, Angus, and Mary Wane (eds), *Thomas Denton: A Perambulation of Cumberland 1678–1688* (Woodbridge: Boydell & Brewer, 2003)

Index

Amory, Thomas 16–17
Appleby 3, 42, 81
Appleby Castle 77
Arne, Thomas 7
Askham 67, 122
Aspatria 51
Atkinson, John 51
Augsburg 60
Avison, Charles 64

Bampton 67
Barbeu-Dubourg, Jacques 54
Barrells Hall, Warwickshire 7
Beckett, J. V. 35, 36
Bicknell, Peter 2, 14, 17
Boerhaave, Herman 51
Bonnie Prince Charlie see *Stuart, Charles Edward*
Borrowdale 59–61, 63–64, 124, 128, 180
Boyd, Charles 78
British Museum 75
Brown, John 14, 17, 63–64
Brownrigg, Mary (née Spedding) 51
Brownrigg, William 23, 43, 50, 51–53, 55, 56, 59, 60, 64, 131, 178
'A Letter to the Author' 26–27
De praxi medica ineunda (1737) 51
The Art of Making Common Salt (1748) 52, 131
Bryam 69, 78
Buckholme 67, 122
Burke, Edmund 62–63
Burn, Richard 3, 17
Burney, Charles 8

Calley, John 44
Camden, William 60–61, 148
Carlisle 41, 51, 78, 159

Carlisle Cathedral 63
Carlyle, Alexander 81
Carter, Elizabeth 12
Castlerigg 59, 180
Charles II 73
Claudian 23, 102, 103
Rape of Proserpina 141, 142
Clerk, Sir John 4, 40, 68–69, 75–77
Cockermouth 1, 5, 56, 127
Cowper, Thomas 14, 61, 174
Crofts, John 18
Crosby Ravensworth 3
Crow Park 65
Cumberland, Richard 64

Dalton, Henry (d.1709) 3, 11
Dalton, John (1709–1763), *works*
adaptation of Milton's *Comus* (1738) 7, 8
Discourses on Several Subjects and Occasions (1757) 9
Epistle to a Young Nobleman from his Preceptor (1736; 1745) 6, 8, 140
Remarks on Twelve Historical Designs of Raphael, and the Museum Graecum et Egyptiacum (1752) 147
Sermon Preach'd at the Abbey-Church at Bath (1745) 9, 140
Sermon Preached before the University of Oxford (1747) 9, 140
Two Sermons Preached before the University of Oxford (1745) 9
Dalton, John (1766–1844) 1
Dalton, John (c.1600–1672) 3, 11
Dalton, John (c.1676–1747) 3, 11
Dalton, Mary (née Clarke) 3, 68
Dalton, Mary (née Gosling) 12, 13
Dalton, Richard 29, 83, 122, 140, 147,

197

From the Mines to the Mountains

148
Davy, Humphrey 19
Dean 1, 3
Defoe, Daniel 18, 148
Denham, John 22
Denman, Derek 65
Denton, Thomas 31, 61
Derwentwater 15, 59, 65, 105, 125
Distington 3, 56
Dixon, Joshua 48
Dodsley, Robert 6, 14
Dublin 35
Dyer, John 6

Eaglesfield 1
Egremont 5
Ellenfoot *see Maryport*

Fairer, David 23
Fiennes, Celia 69, 71
Fisher, Jabez Maud 18, 19
Fitzpatrick, Anne, Countess of Upper Ossory 7
Flatt Hall 34, 36, 37, 42, 81
Foster, Elizabeth 8
Franklin, Benjamin 19, 53–56
Frere, Joan 24

Gale, John 42, 43
Garrick, David 8
George I 77
Gilpin, John Bernard 64
Gilpin, Revd. William (1724–1804) 14, 53, 62, 63
Gilpin, William (1657–1724) 36, 42
Gosling, Francis 12
Gray, Thomas 2, 53

Hobhouse, Henry 16, 19, 47
Hoechstetter, Daniel 60
Holker Hall 80
Holy Trinity Church, Whitehaven 3, 11

Hume, David 5
Hutchinson, William 17, 64

Jackson, William 72
James II 73
Johnson, Samuel 8, 22

Keswick 14, 16, 59–64, 105, 124, 128
Kip, Johannes 71, 76
Knight, Henrietta, Lady Luxborough 7
Knight, Robert 7

Lamplugh, Richard 40
Lawson, Sir Wilfird 61
Le Nôtre, André 73
Leiden 51
Linneaus, Carl 55
Locke, John 68
Lodore 15, 125, 126
Lowther 5, 24, 66–82, 130, 135, 138
Lowther College 3, 4, 68–69, 74, 79
Lowther Hall 14, 68–74, 77, 78, 79, 80
Lowther Park 67, 68, 74–77, 79
Lowther Village 74–76
Lowther, Barbara 11, 25
Lowther, Henry, Baronet of Lowther 24, 69, 77–79, 80, 103–104, 131
Lowther, Hugh (c.1435–1475) 11
Lowther, Hugh (d.1338?) 70
Lowther, Katherine (1735–1809) 11, 25
Lowther, Katherine (née Pennington) (1712–1764) 10, 11, 24, 25–26
Lowther, Lady Mary (née Stuart) 81
Lowther, Margaret 11, 25
Lowther, Richard (1532–1608) 70
Lowther, Robert (1595–1655) 35
Lowther, Robert (1741–1777) 11
Lowther, Robert, Governor of Barbados (1681–1745) 11, 24, 80
Lowther, Sir Christopher, Baronet of Whitehaven (1611–1644) 35

Index

Lowther, Sir Christopher, Baronet of Whitehaven (1666–1731) 39
Lowther, Sir James, Baronet of Whitehaven (1673–1755) 11–12, 27, 28, 31, 39–42, 43, 45, 46, 49, 51, 52, 72, 77, 79, 80, 121
Lowther, Sir James, Earl of Lonsdale (1736–1802) 11, 24, 80–82, 134
Lowther, Sir John (1582–1637) 35, 71
Lowther, Sir John, Baronet of Lowther (1606–1676) 71
Lowther, Sir John, Baronet of Whitehaven (1642–1706) 34, 36, 37, 39, 121
Lowther, Sir John, Viscount Lonsdale (1655–1700) 31, 68, 71, 73, 74, 76
Lowther, Sir Richard (1692–1713) 69, 73, 77
Lowther, William, Baronet of Marske 24, 79
Lyttelton, George 64

Machell, Thomas 74
Marshall, J. D. 42, 43
Maryport 5, 158, 160, 161
Maulds Meaburn 11
Millom 51
Milton, John 7, 8, 16
  L'Allegro (1645) 145
  Comus (1637) 7
  Il Penseroso (1645) 143
  On the Morning of Christ's Nativity (1645) 143
  Paradise Lost (1667; 1674) 16, 21, 143, 144, 145
Myers, Christopher 28

Newcastle 68, 108, 117
Newcomen, Thomas 43, 44
Nicholson, Norman 15
Nicolson, Joseph 3, 17

Ormathwaite 53, 56, 59, 178
Osbaldeston, Richard 27

Patrickson, Thomas 40
Pearch, George 14, 64
Pelham, Charles 80
Pellin, Andrew 37
Pennant, Thomas 2, 18, 19, 28, 55–60
Penrith 77, 79
Percy, Elizabeth, Duchess of Somerset 5
Pitt, William (1759–1806) 81
Ponsonby, John 40
Pope, Alexander 6, 15, 22
  An Essay on Man (1733–1734) 144
  Imitations of Horace (1733–1738) 6
  Rape of the Lock (1712–1717) 15, 141
  Windsor-Forest 22
Pow Beck 31, 35, 36
Preston Isle 36, 45
Pringle, Sir John 53

Queen's College, Oxford 3, 4, 5, 9, 10

Radcliffe, James, Earl of Derwentwater 65
Ravenstonedale 3
Read, Matthias 33–34, 35, 36, 74
Reynolds, Myra 15
Richmond, Joseph 10–11
River Derwent 65, 156, 179, 180
River Eamont 66, 67, 70
River Lowther 24, 66–67, 68, 72, 75, 76, 122
Royal Greenwich Hospital 65
Royal Society, The 45–47, 52, 53

Saltom Pit 45, 47, 54–56
Savery, Thomas 43, 44, 118
Secker, Thomas 10
Senhouse, Humphrey 5, 10

From the Mines to the Mountains

Senhouse, Richard 51
Seymour, Algernon, Earl of Hertford and Duke of Somerset 6, 8, 24
Seymour, Charles, Duke of Somerset 5
Seymour, Frances (née Thynne), Countess of Hertford and Duchess of Somerset 6, 7, 8, 10, 24
Seymour, George, Viscount Beauchamp 5, 6, 8
Shakespeare, William 23
Shap 11, 24, 68
Shap Abbey 67
Shenstone, William 6
Skiddaw 52, 53, 59, 83, 128, 156, 177, 178
Sloane, Sir Hans 52
Smart, Christopher 8
Smirke, Robert 74, 75
Smith, George 60, 62
Smollet, Tobias 9
Smith, Thomas 66
Soulavie, Jean-Louis Giraud 55
Spedding, Carlisle 19, 23, 28, 42, 43–47, 48, 49–51, 111
Spedding, James (1719–1757) 66
Spedding, James (1720–1788) 54, 57
Spedding, John 42–43, 45, 49, 51, 66
Spedding, Thomas (c.1722–1783) 28
St Bees 35, 37, 72, 158, 165 St Bees School 37, 72
St Edmund Hall, Oxford 3
St James' Church, Whitehaven 27–30, 34, 35
St James's Palace 73
St John's in the Vale 62, 127
St Mary-at-Hill, London 6
St Michael's Church, Shap 3
St Nicholas' Church, Whitehaven 35, 37
Stuart, Charles Edward 78
Stukeley, William 44

Talbot, Catherine 12–13
Thomson, James 22
Thorseby, Sir Ralph 38–39, 71
Tickell, Thomas (1657–1724) 36, 72
Tickell, Thomas (1685–1740) 72–74

Verrio, Antonio 69, 73
Virgil 23
   Aeneid 102, 103, 142, 144, 145, 146, 172
Virginia 56, 169
Vitruvius 135–37, 139, 149, 150

Wadd Mines, Borrowdale 60
Walpole, Horace 7, 78
Walpole, Robert 78
Watts, Isaac 6
Weeks, James Eyre 23, 47, 49, 50, 174
Wesley, John 40
West Indies 56
West, Robert 29
West, Thomas 17, 53
Wet Sleddale 67
White, Gilbert 55
Whitehall 73
Whitehaven 12, 14, 18–23, 27–50, 51, 53, 56–59, 72, 77, 79, 81, 102, 107, 121, 131, 162, 165, 168, 171
Wigton 63
Wilkinson, William 3, 68, 79
William III 71, 121
Windsor Castle 73
Worcester 8, 12, 13
Worcester Cathedral 6, 13
Wordsworth, Richard 78
Workington 80, 155, 157, 161, 165, 180
Wyck, Jan 31

Yalden, Thomas 23
Yanwath 67, 122
Young, Arthur 2